QUIET
POWER

QUIET POWER

The Secret Strengths of Introverts

SUSAN CAIN

with GREGORY MONE and ERICA MOROZ

illustrated by GRANT SNIDER

Dial Books for Young Readers

The stories in this book are based on interviews with more than one hundred kids, parents, and teachers. The names of the kids, along with other identifying details, have been changed to protect their privacy.

DIAL BOOKS FOR YOUNG READERS
PENGUIN YOUNG READERS GROUP
An imprint of Penguin Random House LLC
375 Hudson Street
New York, NY 10014

Text copyright © 2016 by Susan Cain
Illustrations copyright © 2016 by Grant Snider

Library of Congress Cataloging-in-Publication Data

Names: Cain, Susan, author. | Mone, Gregory, author. | Snider, Grant, illustrator.
Title: Quiet power : the secret strengths of introverts / Susan Cain with Gregory Mone and Erica Moroz ; illustrated by Grant Snider.
Description: New York : Dial Books, 2016.
Identifiers: LCCN 2015040911 | ISBN 9780803740600 (hardback)
ISBN 9780399186721 (Library binding)
Subjects: LCSH: Introverts—Juvenile literature. | Self-esteem—Juvenile literature. | Interpersonal relations—Juvenile literature. | Families—Juvenile literature. | BISAC: JUVENILE NONFICTION / Social Science / Psychology. | JUVENILE NONFICTION / Social Issues / Self-Esteem & Self-Reliance. | JUVENILE NONFICTION / Social Issues / Emotions & Feelings.
Classification: LCC BF698.35.I59 C356 2016 | DDC 155.4/18232—dc23
LC record available at http://lccn.loc.gov/2015040911

Printed in the United States of America

10 9 8 7 6 5 4 3 2 1

Design by Jasmin Rubero
Text set in Berling LT Std

For Gonzo, Sam, and Eli, with all my love
—S.C.

TABLE OF CONTENTS

✓ 1. A quiet temperament is a hidden superpower.

✓ 2. There's a word for "people who are in their heads too much": thinkers.

✓ 3. Most great ideas spring from solitude.

✓ 4. You can stretch like a rubber band. You can do anything an extrovert can do, including stepping into the spotlight. There will always be time for quiet later.

✓ 5. But even though you'll need to stretch on occasion, you should return to your true self when you're done.

INTROVERTS

✔ 6. Two or three close friends mean more than a hundred acquaintances (though acquaintances are great too).

✔ 7. Introverts and extroverts are yin and yang—we love and need each other.

✔ 8. It's okay to cross the hallway to avoid small talk.

✔ 9. You don't need to be a cheerleader to lead. Just ask Mahatma Gandhi.

✔ 10. Speaking of Gandhi, he said: "In a gentle way, you can shake the world."

QUIET POWER

INTRODUCTION

"Why are you being so quiet?"

Friends, teachers, acquaintances, even people I barely know have asked me this question. Most mean well. They want to know if I'm all right, or if there's a reason that I'm keeping to myself. Some ask in a way that suggests they think it's a little weird that I haven't spoken up in a while.

I don't always have a clear-cut answer to this question. Sometimes I'm quiet because I'm in the middle of a thought or observation. Sometimes I'm more focused on listening than on talking. Often, though, the reason I'm being quiet is because that's just how I am. Quiet.

In school, it always seemed as if "outgoing" was the highest compliment a person could get. In classes, my teachers often asked me to speak up more. At school dances I headed for the dance floor with my friends, but had it been up to me, we would have just hung out together at someone's house. I went along to loud, crowded parties in college, but I couldn't shake the feeling that I would have had a better time eating dinner with a friend or two and going to a movie. I never complained about it, though. I thought that I was supposed to do these things in order to be considered "normal."

Throughout this time, I'd built a small but deep network of close friends and colleagues. I never really cared whether someone was popular or not, which meant that some of my friends were "cool" and others not at all. Thanks to my preference for intimate conversations, my friendships were built on mutual trust, enjoyment of each other's company, and love. They had little to do with cliques or popularity contests. People started to praise me for my insightful questions, my ability to think independently, and my calm approach to tense situations. They complimented me on being a deep thinker and great listener. They also started listening to *me*. They noticed that when I spoke, it was because I had something thoughtful to say. And once I moved into the working world, the bold, outspoken types who had once intimidated me started offering me jobs!

As time went on, I realized that my quiet approach to life had been a great power all along. It was a tool that I'd just needed to learn how to use. I looked around and saw that many of the great contributions to the world—from the Apple computer to the Cat in the Hat—had been made by introverts because of, not in spite of, their quiet temperaments. I culled my ideas into a book for adults called *Quiet: The Power of Introverts in a World That Can't Stop Talking*. It hit the *New York Times* best seller list and has stayed there for years, and has been translated into forty languages. Thousands and thousands of people have told me that this simple idea—that their quiet approach, if used correctly, is a powerful force—actually changed their lives. It touched them in ways I could not have imagined.

Soon I was doing things that seemed impossible when I was younger. When I was in middle school, for example, I was terrified of public speaking. I couldn't sleep the night before I had to give a book report. One time I was so scared that I froze up in front of everyone and couldn't even open my mouth. Now, as an advocate for introverted people, I appear on screens all over the world and deliver lectures in front of thousands of people. I gave a TED Talk about introversion that became one of the most watched TED Talks of all time, with many millions of views. ("TED" stands for technology, entertainment, and design, and is the name of an organization that holds conferences where people share big ideas.)

Inspired by these experiences, I cofounded Quiet Revolution, a mission-based company whose goal is to empower introverts of all ages. I want us quiet types to feel we can be ourselves wherever we are—at school, at work, and in society at large. Quiet Revolution advocates for change and boosts the voices of us introverts. The movement is inclusive—*anyone* is allowed to join, no matter how quiet or outgoing they are. I encourage you to get involved on Quietrev.com!

People often ask me whether I've turned into an extrovert, now that I'm such a comfortable public speaker and media commentator. But I haven't changed in any fundamental way over the years. I still feel shy sometimes. And I love my quiet, reflective self. I've embraced the power of quiet—and you can too.

Many of my readers have told me they wish they'd heard about the Quiet Revolution when they were kids, or when they were parents raising their own introverted children. And I've also heard from inspiring young people who wish that there was a version of *Quiet* just for them.

That's where this book comes in.

WHAT'S AN INTROVERT, ANYWAY?

There's a psychological term for people like me. We're called introverts—and there's no single way to define us. We enjoy the company of others but also like time alone. We can have great social skills, and also be private and keep to ourselves. We are observant. We might listen more than we talk. Being an introvert is about having a deep inner life, and considering that inner life to be important.

If an introvert is someone who looks inward, an extrovert is just the opposite. Extroverts thrive in groups and gain energy from being around others. Even if you aren't an introvert yourself, there are probably a few of us in your family or your circle of friends. Introverts make up a third to half of the population—that's one out of every two or three people you know. Sometimes we're easy to spot. We're the ones curled up on the sofa with a book or an iPad on our lap instead of surrounded by people. At crowded parties you might find us talking to a handful of friends—definitely not dancing on the table. In class, we sometimes look away when the teacher searches for volunteers. We're paying attention—we'd just prefer to follow along quietly and to contribute when we're ready.

Other times, we introverts are pretty good at hiding our true natures. We might pass undetected in classrooms and school cafeterias, living out loud when deep down we can't wait to escape the crowd and to have some time to ourselves. Ever since I published my book, I've been amazed by how many seemingly extroverted people—including actors, politicians, entrepreneurs, and athletes—have "confessed" to me that they are introverts too.

Being introverted doesn't necessarily mean being shy. This is an important distinction. Introverts *can* be shy, of course, but there's such a thing as a shy extrovert too. Shy behavior can look like introversion—it makes people appear to be quiet and reserved. Like introversion, the feeling of shyness is complicated; it has a lot of layers to it. It can come from a place of nervousness, or insecurity, about being accepted by others. It can come from a place of fear of doing the wrong thing. In class, a shy student might not raise his hand because he's worried about giving the incorrect answer and feeling embarrassed. The introverted girl sitting next to him might keep her hand down too, but for different reasons. Maybe she doesn't feel the need to contribute. Or she might be too busy listening and processing everything to talk. Just like introversion, shyness has its advantages. Studies show that shy kids tend to have loyal friendships, and to be conscientious, empathetic, and creative. Both shy and introverted people make great listeners. And it's through listening that we tend to be good at observing, learning, and maturing.

This book is about *both* introversion and shyness—and about the advantages both qualities give you. I happen to be an introvert and a naturally shy person (even though I have come to feel less shy with time). But you might be only one or the other. Take the parts of the book that apply to you, and don't worry about the rest.

ARE *YOU* AN INTROVERT, EXTROVERT, OR AMBIVERT?

Psychology is the study of human behavior and the human mind and its functions. Of course, each person's mind has its own special wiring, but everyone follows more or less the same framework, and there's a lot of overlap between us all. Carl Jung (pronounced "young"), a famous twentieth-century psychologist, introduced the terms "introvert" and "extrovert" as a way to describe different personality types. Jung was an introvert himself, and he was the first to explain that introverts are drawn to the inner world of thoughts and feelings, while their opposites, extroverts, crave the external world of people and activities.

Of course, even Jung said that no one is all introvert or all extrovert. These traits exist on what's called a spectrum. The best way to understand a spectrum is to imagine a long ruler. Let's say there are extreme extroverts at one end of the ruler, and extreme introverts at the other. There are people who fall near the middle—psychologists call them "ambiverts"—but even those who tend toward one of the two sides are still a bit of a mix. Many introverts say that when they're with close friends or discussing an interesting subject, they act more like extroverts. And as much as extroverts like to be around people, most of them also need downtime to chill out too.

Before we go any further, here's the chance to see where you fall on the introvert-extrovert spectrum. There are no right or wrong answers. Just pick "true" or "false" based on which one most often applies to you.

- ○ I prefer spending time with one or two friends instead of a group.
- ○ I'd rather express my ideas in writing.
- ○ I enjoy being alone.
- ○ I prefer deep conversations to small talk.
- ○ My friends tell me that I'm a good listener.
- ○ I prefer small classes to large ones.
- ○ I avoid conflicts.
- ○ I don't like showing people my work until it's perfect.
- ○ I work best on my own.
- ○ I don't like being called on in class.
- ○ I feel drained after hanging out with friends, even when I have fun.
- ○ I'd rather celebrate my birthday with a few friends and family, instead of having a huge party.
- ○ I don't mind big independent projects at school.
- ○ I spend lots of time in my room.
- ○ I'm usually not a big risk taker.
- ○ I can dive into a project, practice a sport or instrument, or engage in something creative for hours at a time, without getting bored.
- ○ I tend to think before I speak.

○ I'd rather text or e-mail than talk on the phone with someone I don't know very well.

○ I don't feel totally comfortable being the center of attention.

○ I usually like asking questions more than I like answering them.

○ People often describe me as soft-spoken or shy.

○ If I had to choose, I'd prefer a weekend with absolutely nothing to do to one with too many things scheduled.

This is an informal quiz, not a scientifically validated personality test. The questions were formulated based on characteristics of introversion often accepted by contemporary researchers.

The more often you answered "true," the more introverted you probably are. If you answered "false" more often, it's likely you're more of an extrovert. If you answered "true" and "false" equally, you're probably an ambivert.

Whichever way you lean is fine. The key to a comfortable life is to know your own preferences. Some people really are "born introverts" or "born extroverts," and personality traits like introversion and extroversion can be passed down from one generation to the next. Our genes don't decide everything, though. Even if you see yourself as one or the other, your personality and attitude aren't set in stone; you have lots of room to shape and develop them over time. Someone born with an extremely shy and quiet temperament probably won't grow up to perform in front of stadiums like Taylor Swift, but most of us can stretch to some degree, much the way a rubber band can stretch very flexibly (up to a certain point).

Recognizing which kinds of situations make you feel masterful and at ease can give you a sense of control. Then you can make choices based on what you know works for you. You can pursue the activities that bring you comfort—and step outside your comfort zone when you feel it's worthwhile, for the sake of a project or person you care about. I can't emphasize enough how empowering it is to live this way—so we'll come back to this point throughout the book. Validation from those around you—online or in person—feels good, but the most important validation comes from your very own self.

EXTROVERTS ARE GREAT TOO

Society often overlooks us introverts. We idolize the talkers and the spotlight seekers, as if they are the role models *everyone* should be emulating. I call this the Extrovert Ideal. This is the belief that we're all supposed to be quick-thinking, charismatic risk takers who prefer action to contemplation. The Extrovert Ideal is what can make you feel as if there's something wrong with you because you're not at your best in a large group. It's an especially powerful force in school, where the loudest, most talkative kids are often the most popular, and where teachers reward the students who are eager to raise their hands in class.

This book questions the Extrovert Ideal—but that doesn't mean it questions extroverts themselves. My best friend, Judith, is a social butterfly who has been at the center of the "popular crowd" since elementary school. My beloved husband, Ken, is a charming take-charge type who always has interesting stories to share in a group. I love Judith and Ken partly *because* we're different, and we complement each other. They see strengths in me that they don't have themselves (or don't have as often as they would like), and I feel the exact same way about them.

I really can't say enough about the yin and yang of the two personality types. When we join together, we're so much better than the sum of our two parts. My husband and I use a Mexican expression to describe this: "*juntos somos más,*" which in English means "together we are more."

As much as I love extroverts, though, I want to shine the spotlight on what it feels like to be quiet—and to show just how powerful quiet can be. It's no accident that many of history's greatest artists, inventors, scientists, athletes, and business leaders were introverts. As a child, Mahatma Gandhi was shy and afraid of everything, especially other people; he used to run home from school as soon as the bell rang, to avoid socializing with his classmates. But he grew up to lead the nation of India to freedom, without changing his fundamental nature. He fought his battles through peaceful, nonviolent protests.

The National Basketball Association's all-time leading scorer, Kareem Abdul-Jabbar, would toss his sky hooks in front of tens of thousands of people each night, but he enjoyed neither the crowds nor the attention. He loved reading history books and described himself as a nerd who happened to be good at basketball. He's also used his quiet time to write, publishing both novels and memoirs.

What about Beyoncé? You may know this icon for her sold-out stadium shows around the world. Or for her music videos, which, combined, have garnered over a billion YouTube views. But even though Beyoncé grew up performing from an early age, she describes herself as an introverted child. Now her confidence inspires her fans around the world—but it doesn't mean that she has changed her quiet, observant ways. "I'm a good listener and I like to observe, and sometimes people think that's being shy," she says.

The gifted actress Emma Watson is a shy introvert too. "The truth is that I'm genuinely a shy, socially awkward, introverted person," says Watson. "At a big party . . . it's too much stimulation for me, which is why I end up going to the bathroom! I need time-outs. . . . I'm terrible at small talk. . . . I feel a pressure when I'm meeting new people because I'm aware of their expectations. Which isn't to say that when I'm in a small group and around my friends, I don't love to dance and be extroverted. I am just extremely self-conscious in public."

Misty Copeland has been touted as an "unlikely ballerina." Like most athletes, she started training young—but not nearly as young as most ballerinas, who often start as early as age four! As a shy thirteen-year-old, Misty thought that her middle-school audition for the drill team had been a bust. But even though she was quiet, she didn't go unnoticed. Her strength and talent were undeniable, and her ability to observe and focus on complex choreography was unique for someone her age. She was named captain of the squad of sixty girls that day, eventually leading her on the path to ballet. In 2015, she became the first black female principal dancer in American Ballet Theatre's history.

Albert Einstein is another well-known introvert. As a child, his preference for independent learning sometimes got him in trouble. When he was sixteen, he failed a school entrance exam partly because he hadn't taken the time to study all the subjects; he'd focused only on what interested him. Later, though, he learned to mix his intense periods of solitary work with small social gatherings. In his twenties, he started the Olympia Academy, a club where he'd meet with a few close friends to discuss the ideas he'd spent so many hours developing in solitude. When he was twenty-six years old, Einstein completely rewrote the laws of physics. At age forty-two, he won the Nobel Prize.

In the following pages, you'll meet quiet kids who excel at traditionally introverted activities, such as writing and art. You'll also meet introverts who are presidents of their school class, champion public speakers, athletes, actors, and singers. These roles might not seem suited to quiet kids—and in many cases, the kids I'll introduce you to were reluctant to pursue them at first. But they drove themselves forward out of passion for their work. This single-minded passion is a common characteristic of many introverts—I hope that over time (it doesn't have to happen right away) you'll identify your own!

Through the stories and experiences of other young people like you, I'll address questions that introverts often wonder about. How do you carve out a place for yourself as a quiet person? How can you make sure that you're not ignored? And how do you make new friends when it feels hard to muster the confidence to be chatty?

In this book we'll talk about the ways we introverts relate to those around us—to friends, family, and teachers. We'll talk about the ways we pursue our interests and hobbies. And we'll talk about the ways we relate to our own selves, as individuals. I hope that through this book you learn to accept and treasure yourself—just as you are. The world needs you, and there are so many ways to make your quiet style speak volumes.

Think of this as a guide book. It won't teach you how to turn yourself into someone else. Instead, it will teach you to use the marvelous qualities and skills you *already* have. And then . . . look out, world!

PART ONE
SCHOOL

Chapter One
QUIET IN THE CAFETERIA

When I was nine years old, I convinced my parents to let me go to summer camp for eight weeks. My parents were skeptical, but I couldn't wait to get there. I'd read lots of novels set at summer camps on wooded lakes, and it sounded like so much fun.

Before I left, my mother helped me pack a suitcase full of shorts, sandals, swimsuits, towels, and . . . books. Lots and lots and lots of books. This made perfect sense to us; reading was a group activity in our family. At night and on weekends, my parents, siblings, and I would all sit around the living room and disappear into our novels. There wasn't much talking. Each of us would follow our own fictional adventures, but in our way we were sharing this time together. So when my mother packed me all those novels, I pictured the same kind of experience at camp, only better. I could see myself and all my new friends in our cabin: ten girls in matching nightgowns reading together happily.

But I was in for a big surprise. Summer camp turned out to be the exact *opposite* of quiet time with my family. It was more like one long, raucous birthday party—and I couldn't even phone my parents to take me home.

On the very first day of camp, our counselor gathered us together. In the name of camp spirit, she said, she would demonstrate a cheer that we were to perform every day for the rest of the summer. Pumping her arms at her sides as if she were jogging, the counselor chanted:

"R-O-W-D-I-E,

THAT'S THE WAY

WE SPELL ROWDY,

ROWDIE! ROWDIE!

LET'S GET ROWDIE!"

She finished with both her hands up, palms out, and a huge smile on her face.

Okay, this was *not* what I was expecting. I was already excited to be at camp—why the need to be so outwardly rowdy? (And why did we have to spell this word incorrectly?!) I wasn't sure what to think. Gamely I performed the cheer— and then found some downtime to pull out one of my books and start reading.

Later that week, though, the coolest girl in the bunk asked me why I was always reading and why I was so "mellow"— mellow being the opposite of R-O-W-D-I-E. I looked down at the book in my hand, then around the bunk. No one else was sitting by herself, reading. They were all laughing and playing hand games, or running around in the grass outside with kids from other bunks. So I closed my book and put it away, along with all the others, in my suitcase. I felt guilty as I tucked the books under my bed, as if they needed me and I was letting them down.

For the rest of the summer, I shouted out the ROWDIE cheer with as much enthusiasm as I could muster. Every day I pumped my arms and smiled wide, doing my best approximation of a lively, gregarious camper. And when camp was over and I finally reunited with my books, something felt different. It felt as if, at school and even with my friends, that pressure to be rowdy still loomed large.

In elementary school, I'd known everyone since kindergarten. I knew I was shy deep down, but I felt very comfortable and had even starred in the school play one year. Everything changed in middle school, though, when I switched to a new school system where I didn't know anyone. I was the new kid in a sea of chattering strangers. My mom would drive me to school because being on a bus with dozens of other kids was too overwhelming. The doors to the school stayed locked until the first bell, and when I arrived early I'd have to wait outside in the parking lot, where groups of friends huddled together.

They all seemed to know one another and to feel totally at ease. For me, that parking lot was a straight-up nightmare.

Eventually, the bell would ring and we'd rush inside. The hallways were even more chaotic than the parking lot. Kids hurried in every direction, pounding down the hall like they owned the place, and groups of girls and boys traded stories and laughed secretively. I'd look up at a vaguely familiar face, wonder if I should say hello, and then move on without speaking.

But the cafeteria scene at lunchtime made the hallways look like a dream! The voices of hundreds of kids bounced off the massive cinderblock walls. The room was arranged in rows of long, skinny tables, and a laughing, gabbing clique sat at each one. Everyone split off into groups: the shiny, popular girls here, the athletic boys there, the nerdy types over to the side. I could barely think straight, let alone smile and chat in the easygoing way that everyone else seemed to manage.

Does this setting sound familiar? It's such a common experience.

Meet Davis, a thoughtful and shy guy who found himself in a similar situation on the first day of sixth grade. As one of the few Asian American kids at a mostly white school, he was also made uncomfortably aware that other students thought he looked "different." He was so nervous that he barely remembered to exhale until he arrived in homeroom, where everyone gradually settled down. Finally, he could just sit and think. The rest of the day went on similarly—he barely navigated his way through the crowded cafeteria, feeling relieved only during quiet moments in the classroom. By the time the bell rang at 3:30 p.m., he was exhausted. He had made it through the first day of sixth grade alive—though not without somebody throwing gum into his hair on the bus ride home.

As far as he could tell, everyone seemed thrilled to be back again the next morning. Everyone except Davis.

INTROVERTS AND THE FIVE SENSES

Things started looking up, though, in ways Davis could never have imagined on that stressful first day. I'll tell you the rest of his story soon. In the meantime, it's important to remember that no matter how cheerful they might have seemed, the kids at my school and at Davis's probably weren't *all* happy to be there. The first days in a new school, or even one you've been going to for years, can be a struggle for anyone. And as introverts, our reactivity to stimulation means that people like Davis and me really *do* have extra adjustments to make.

What do I mean by "reactivity to stimulation"? Well, most psychologists agree that introversion and extroversion are among the most important personality traits shaping human experience—and that this is true of people all over the world, regardless of their culture or the language they speak. This means that introversion is also one of the most *researched* personality traits. We're learning fascinating things about it every day. We now know, for example, that introverts and extroverts generally have different nervous systems. Introverts' nervous systems react more intensely than extroverts' to social situations as well as to sensory experiences. Extroverts' nervous systems don't react as much, which means that they crave stimulation, such as brighter lights and louder sounds, to feel alive. When they're not getting enough stimulation, they may start to feel bored and antsy. They naturally prefer a more gregarious, or chatty, style of socializing. They *need* to be around people, and they thrive on the energy of crowds. They're more likely to crank up speakers, chase adrenaline-pumping adventures, or thrust their hands up and volunteer to go first.

We introverts, on the other hand, react more—sometimes much, much more—to stimulating environments such as noisy school cafeterias. This means that we tend to feel most relaxed and energized when we're in quieter settings—not necessarily alone, but often with smaller numbers of friends or family we know well.

In one study, a famous psychologist named Hans Eysenck placed lemon juice—a stimulant—on the tongues of adult introverts and extroverts. The human mouth's natural response to a burst of lemon juice is to produce saliva, which balances out the acidic citrus taste. So, Eysenck figured he could measure sensitivity to stimulation—in this case the stimulation of a drop of lemon juice—by measuring how much saliva each person produced in response to the liquid. He guessed that the introverts would be more sensitive to the lemon juice and generate more saliva. And he was right.

In a similar study, scientists found that infants who are more sensitive to the sweet taste of sugar water are more likely to grow up to be teenagers who are sensitive to the noise of a loud party. We simply feel the effects of taste, sound, and social life a little more intensely than our extroverted counterparts.

Other experiments have yielded similar results. The psychologist Russell Geen gave introverts and extroverts math problems to solve, with varying levels of background noise playing as they worked. He found that the introverts performed better when the background noise was quieter, while the extroverts did fine with the louder sounds.

This is one reason that introverts like Davis tend to prefer being around just a few people at a time; it's less overwhelming than being surrounded by many different people at once. At parties, for example, we introverts can have a fantastic time, but sometimes we run out of energy sooner and wish we could leave early. Spending time alone in quiet settings recharges introverts' batteries. That's why we often enjoy solo activities, from reading to running to mountain climbing. Don't let anyone tell you that introverts are antisocial—we are just *differently* social.

Thriving at school or anywhere else comes more naturally when you're in an environment that allows your nervous system to function at its best. And the fact is, most schools are not environments for introverts' nervous systems. But once you start paying attention to the messages your body is sending you—such as feeling anxious or overwhelmed—the power is in your hands. You've recognized that something feels off, and now you know that a change needs to be made. You can take action to find your equilibrium—even before you get back to the sanctuary of your room at home. You can listen to your body and seek out the quiet spots in your school to collect yourself, such as a library or computer lab or the empty classroom of a friendly teacher. You can even duck into the restroom to have a moment to yourself!

Davis probably understood this intuitively; that's why after the gum incident, he started sitting at the front of the bus, where no one bothered him. He tried to tune out the rip-roaring sounds of games and phones beeping and of kids shouting and laughing. Soon enough, he found a pair of earplugs and used the bus time to read. He plowed through the whole Harry Potter series and turned to self-improvement books, like *The Seven Habits of Highly Effective Teens* and *How to Win Friends and Influence People*. Shutting out the noise was his way of reducing stimulation and keeping his head clear.

SUPPOSED TO?

There's a lot to figure out as we move through adolescence. Our physical, emotional, and social needs are all going in new directions, and it can feel as if these needs have been tossed into a blender and remixed into something different. It's both scary *and* exciting. While you're navigating the social sea, remember that even your more extroverted friends are working through social insecurities of their own. Adolescent insecurity is something we *all* go through—even if we have an older sibling to show us the ropes, or have watched lots of movies about high school, or have been popular since kindergarten.

Julian, a charismatic high school senior from Brooklyn, New York, who loves photography, remembers feeling frustrated that being quiet meant getting less attention from kids in his grade. "I used to be pretty weird," he remarks with a laugh. "In elementary school and the start of middle school, I was ashamed of how quiet I was, so I used to try to get attention in other ways, like putting stuff down people's shirts, stealing people's pens—stuff like that. I'd come home and not feel very good. Now I've calmed down. I try to connect to people, not to annoy them. I don't put up all the fronts that I used to."

Karinah, a reserved fifteen-year-old also from Brooklyn, often feels anxious when she's forced into social settings. While Julian used to make up for his introversion by being loud or annoying, Karinah has felt stuck in her own head for as long as she can remember. "When I'm socializing, even with someone I know from school, I feel like I just want to be normal. I don't want to say the wrong thing, and I don't always say what's on my mind; I can't always word it properly."

Dr. Chelsea Grefe, a New York–based psychologist, has some thoughts about what someone in Karinah's shoes can do to prepare for these kinds of situations. Dr. Grefe recalls meeting a bright and artistically gifted fifth grader who was nervous about making conversation with other kids. The girl wanted to expand her social horizons. She had two really good friends at school but felt lost when she was separated from them. Dr. Grefe encouraged the girl to brainstorm before entering situations she knew would be uncomfortable. "It was about making a plan and role-playing how to initiate conversations," she says. First, Karinah identified girls in other groups whom she felt comfortable approaching. Then she set herself a goal: to ask them one-on-one if they wanted to sit together or hang out later. This pre-planning allowed her to avoid approaching a cafeteria table full of people with no clue what to say.

Dr. Grefe suggests coming up with some conversation starters, even simple ones such as: "What did you do this weekend?" or "Are you getting excited for this particular school event?" This way, you're prepared as you enter a social situation and have something to fall back on.

Maggie, a college student from Pennsylvania, used to compare herself to other kids in her class—the bubbly ones, the "natural leaders." She often wondered why the popular kids were so popular. Some of them weren't even that well liked! Sometimes they were the most attractive, or athletic, or smart, but often it seemed more about how outgoing they were. They were the ones talking to whomever they wanted, or shouting out in class, or throwing parties. These were *not* qualities that she had, and sometimes she felt ignored—or weird—because of it.

"When all the loud kids or popular kids were talking and

laughing, I'd feel like, 'Ugh, why can't I just join in their conversation? It's not a big deal! What is wrong with me?'" After all, Maggie was funny and kind. She had things to say. But at school, she didn't show off these qualities, so she felt unnoticed and underappreciated.

I'm happy to report that Maggie's perspective changed over time. When she found out that she wasn't the only introvert "in the entire universe," it was a huge relief. "It started to come together when I read *The Outsiders* by S. E. Hinton in seventh grade," Maggie said. "The first page of that book really stuck with me. The main character, Ponyboy, is walking home from a movie by himself, and he says that sometimes he just prefers to 'lone it.' I was so surprised and happy to read those words. It made me realize that this was a *thing*! Others feel this way too!"

As I said earlier, a third to a half of the human population is introverted. Being introverted is not something to outgrow; it is something to accept and grow *into*—and even to cherish. The more you notice how special your introverted qualities are—and how some of the things you like best about yourself are probably connected to your introverted nature—the more your confidence will flourish and spread to other areas of your life. You don't have to pick the activity, or befriend the people, you think you're *supposed* to. Instead, do what you enjoy, and pick friends whose company you truly value.

A girl named Ruby told me that during high school she twisted herself into a pretzel trying to be a gregarious "freshman mentor," because that was a prestigious role at her school. Only after she was kicked out of the program for not being outgoing enough did she realize that actually she preferred science. She started spending time after school working with her biology teacher, and she eventually published her first scientific paper at the age of seventeen. She even won a university scholarship for biomedical engineering!

As Ruby's story shows us, there are all kinds of things that we really should do as good people, like being kind or helpful to our friends and families. But there are also so many *supposed to*'s. In my first year of middle school, I struggled to be the outgoing version of myself I thought I was supposed to be: bubbly, cool, and loud. It took me time to realize that I could just be whoever I was naturally. After all, the people I looked up to—my heroes and role models—were writers. They seemed genuinely cool to me—and most of them also happened to be introverts. Even though back then I didn't have the benefit of understanding my nervous system, or even a word to describe my personality, I eventually started adapting my social life to its needs. I made some really great friends, and I noticed that I wanted to hang out with them one or two at a time, not in big groups. I decided that I wasn't going to have the largest number of friendships, but I *was* going to have plenty of deep and excellent ones. And I've continued doing that all my life.

AN ANIMATED EXPLANATION

I've come to realize not only how important it is to follow my instincts and interests, but also to express my feelings and explain my actions to others. Here's an example that might be familiar to you: Say you're walking through the hallway, from one class to another, deep in thought or possibly overwhelmed by the noise and crowds. You pass a friend or classmate and glance at her briefly, but you're so preoccupied that you don't manage to stop to say hi and chitchat. You haven't meant to be rude or hurtful, but your friend thinks you're angry about something.

Be on the lookout for moments of misunderstanding such as this one, and do your best to explain what you were thinking and feeling. An extroverted friend—and maybe even an introverted one—likely won't guess that you were distracted by your thoughts or by too much sensory stimulation, and your explanation will make all the difference.

Not everyone will understand your nature, though, even if you try to explain it. When Robby, a teenager from New Hampshire, first learned about introversion, he felt a great sense of relief. He had a tendency to turn quiet in large groups, and although he'd always felt comfortable talking and joking with his closest friends, he had a limit. "After a couple of hours I'm like, 'Whoa, I can't do this.' It's draining. There's a wall that goes up and I don't want to talk to anyone. It's not physical exhaustion. It's *mental* exhaustion."

Robby tried to explain the differences between introverts and extroverts to an outgoing friend, but she couldn't understand his perspective. She thrived in loud, busy places and didn't see why he needed to be alone so often. Another friend of his, Drew, grasped the idea immediately. Drew was more of an ambivert. He wasn't as outgoing as his younger sister, but he wasn't as reserved as his parents, either. The more he talked with Robby about what it was like to be introverted, the more he wanted people to understand both sides of his own personality.

As an amateur filmmaker, Drew had been experimenting with a new animation style, and after researching the subject of introversion, he produced an animated, graphics-intensive public service announcement about what it means to be quiet. Drew posted it on YouTube, but that was only the start. He was also a producer of the high school's television news show. Once a week, every student in the school watched the latest episode, and in one of these Drew included his PSA on introverts. The response was overwhelming; even one of the teachers, who was secretly introverted, expressed his gratitude. "I was able to bring the whole school community to an understanding," Drew said. "For weeks afterward, people would come up to me and say, 'Hey, that was awesome!'" His friend Robby thanked him more than anyone.

Every school could benefit from a deeper understanding of the different strengths and needs of introverted and extroverted students. The middle and high school years are the most difficult times to be introverted, because when hundreds of kids are crammed together in a single building it can feel as if the only way to gain respect and friendship is through vivacity and visibility. But there are so many other great qualities to have, such as the ability to focus deeply on topics and activities, and a talent for listening with empathy and patience. These are two of the "superpowers" of introverts. Channel them; find your passions and pursue them wholeheartedly. Then you will not only survive but also *thrive*.

STANDING OUT QUIETLY

Sometimes it's natural for the stress and drama of the school day to get to you. But you *can* rise above all that with your inner self intact. Here are a few quick tips that you can always refer back to:

UNDERSTAND YOUR NEEDS: The boisterous environments common to schools are often taxing to introverts. Acknowledge that sometimes there will be a mismatch between you and your environment, but try not to let it stop you from being you. Find quiet times and places to recharge your batteries. And if you prefer to socialize with one or two friends at a time, rather than in a big group, that's just fine! It can be a relief to find people who feel the same way, or who just understand where you're coming from.

LOOK FOR YOUR OWN CIRCLE: You may find that your sweet spot is with athletes, coders, or with people who are just plain nice whether or not your interests are perfectly aligned. If you need to make a checklist of things to talk about in order to get a friendship rolling, go for it.

COMMUNICATE: Make sure your closest friends understand why you retreat or become quiet at times during school; talk to them about introversion and extroversion. If they're extroverts, ask them what *they* need from you.

FIND YOUR PASSION: This is crucial to everyone, regardless of personality type, but it's especially important for introverts, because many of us like to focus our energy on one or two projects we really care about. Also, when you're feeling scared, genuine passion will lift you up and give you the excitement you need to propel you through your fear. Fear is a powerful enemy, but passion is an even stronger friend.

EXPAND YOUR COMFORT ZONE: We can all stretch to some degree, pushing past our apparent limitations in the service of a cause or a passion project. And if you're stretching into an area that really frightens you—for many people, public speaking falls into this category—make sure to practice in small, manageable steps. You'll read more about this in chapter 13.

KNOW YOUR BODY LANGUAGE: Smiling will not only make other people comfortable around you—it will also make you happier and more confident. This is a biological phenomenon: Smiling sends a signal to the rest of your body that all is well. But this principle is not just about smiles: Pay attention to what your body does when you're feeling confident and at ease—and what it does when you feel tense. Crossing your arms, for example, is often a reaction to nervousness, and it can make you seem—and feel—closed off. Practice arranging your body in the positions that don't signal distress—and that make it feel good.

Chapter Two
QUIET IN THE CLASSROOM

Every four weeks, Grace would burst through the door of her house after school, annoyed beyond belief. "Again!" she would vent to her mom. It happened each time the eighth-grade Student of the Month award was announced. The award was given for hard work, good behavior, and general class participation, but as far as Grace could tell, it was always handed to one of the outgoing kids. The winners, Grace explained, were always the ones who raised their hands constantly. That just wasn't Grace's style. In class, she sat in the back and followed the discussion by listening and jotting down notes. Other kids would blurt out a string of words at any opportunity. To her, it didn't even seem like they were thinking before they raised their hands. It seemed as if they just wanted an audience.

Grace's teachers encouraged her to contribute more. Her friendly English teacher could tell from her written assignments that she had things to add to class discussions, and she would often prompt Grace to speak up. "She would say to me sometimes, 'Grace, you're being really quiet. How about you read the next three paragraphs in the textbook?'" Reluctantly, Grace would.

After months of not getting the recognition she felt she deserved, Grace was set on winning that award. Her grades were good enough and she never caused trouble in class. Even though she shied away from the spotlight, she still wanted to be noticed. So she decided to mix things up: Whenever one of her teachers asked for volunteers to read aloud, Grace started raising her hand immediately. If she thought her voice sounded too shaky, she'd stop after one paragraph. If she felt good, she'd keep going. She also vowed to contribute more to open class discussions.

Grace started to notice patterns to her nervousness. For example, she felt less anxious when she was called on about halfway through the class, after some of her peers had already spoken. That way, she'd have a chance to formulate her own opinions; she could either expand on other students' ideas or disagree with them and propose something new. Sometimes when she was called on to answer a question first, she'd offer to go second or third instead, to give herself a little extra time to craft an answer. Then she'd suggest another student, some-one who looked eager to have his or her voice heard.

It was nerve-racking, but the strategy worked. Grace forced up her hand more and more, slowly but surely. She volun-teered to read, asked questions when she needed clarifica-tion, and offered her opinions in class discussions. She hadn't changed her ways, exactly—it was more that they were evolving out of her natural habits. Before long, she was awarded Student of the Month.

RETHINKING CLASS PARTICIPATION

Class participation has its benefits—it can be fun to express your ideas aloud, and it's definitely a skill you'll need throughout life—but in my opinion, some teachers push the idea of participation too far. Brianna, a Colorado teenager, had a teacher who gave each student three Popsicle sticks at the start of every class. The kids would sit in a big circle, and whenever they added something to the class discussion, they would throw one of their Popsicle sticks into the center. By the end of the class, they were supposed to have gotten rid of all of their sticks. "If all three sticks weren't gone, your grade would go down dramatically," Brianna recalled.

Instead of enriching the discussion, said Brianna, the Popsicle stick technique led to meaningless blather. Kids spoke up just to be able to throw a stick into the center. Brianna too had to stoop to this level, and it frustrated her. "I don't like to talk just to talk," she said. "If I have something important to say, I will. But I ended up just saying a quick little sentence about anything so I could throw in the stick."

Other teachers grade students on class participation, awarding higher grades to vocal students, whether or not they've mastered the subject. But there are methods of teaching that instead measure "classroom engagement"—a much broader concept than "participation" that makes room for lots of different ways of interacting with material.

Group discussion in class makes sense for a few reasons. It allows students to hear others' ideas, and it reveals to teachers whether students are doing their work and whether they find it challenging. A strong class discussion can be a great way to keep students engaged with the material. But the key word is *engaged*. A quiet student who says little to nothing could be just as engaged as an outgoing one who tosses out responses effortlessly.

A researcher named Mary Budd Rowe once studied how long teachers wait between asking a question and calling on a student who has raised his or her hand. She made video recordings of classroom discussions, studied the results, and found that teachers wait, on average, about one second before calling on someone. One second!

Some educators are trying to improve class discussions by introducing a concept called "think time," or as Rowe called it, "wait time." It goes like this: After the teacher asks a question, he or she allows students a silent minute or two to think before continuing the discussion.

A similar technique is "Think/Pair/Share," in which students first sit quietly and think, then express their ideas to one peer or to a small group. Only then do they return to a whole-class discussion. This is a way to slowly expand your audience and ease you into feeling comfortable sharing. It also allows you time to reflect and to develop your thoughts.

If you aren't lucky enough to have a teacher who embraces ideas such as think time, and you believe your teacher would be receptive, you might try to summon the courage to have a discussion with her or him. Here's the story of a girl in England named Emily who did just that. Emily was quiet in large groups but loud with her friends, and she learned about some of the ideas in this book through my talks and articles. When she was twelve, she had a teacher who had been calling her out for not participating enough. The idea of actually going up to her teacher and explaining herself directly was too intimidating. So instead, Emily wrote him a note. She explained that she was introverted, and that it made her uncomfortable to speak in front of such a large group. Later, her teacher asked her to stay after class for a talk. It turned out that he was an introvert too. He understood why Emily was so reluctant to speak up in class, and promised to create more opportunities for her to work in smaller groups.

By communicating your needs, just as Emily did when she wrote to her teacher, you let others know where you're coming from. Emily's note allowed her teacher to understand that she wasn't bored or disinterested in class; she just felt uncomfortable speaking up in front of the group.

Calling attention to your shy or introverted ways may sound like a contradiction, but Emily's story goes to show that you don't have to suffer alone. Others can take steps to help you feel more comfortable—and they might even know these feelings from their own experiences.

HOW TO BE HEARD IN THE CLASSROOM

As much as I'd like to see schools and teachers rethink their approach to class participation, I also believe that you'll feel more satisfied over the long run if you develop the confidence to contribute your ideas verbally, instead of bottling them up. Your ideas deserve to be heard and appreciated. In fact, one study found that in the typical group setting, introverts' contributions become more and more appreciated over time, because others realize that when introverts raise their hands to speak, they usually have something worthwhile to say.

If you're a reluctant class participator, it may be helpful to understand *why* you feel so much discomfort speaking in class. This knowledge can make it easier to develop strategies, as Grace did, for sharing your ideas on your own terms.

Why does speaking up feel so unnatural? Here are a few of the common reasons we've heard:

I don't want to be wrong.

I don't want to say something meaningless.

I'm too busy listening to talk.

I don't have enough time to think up a response.

I'm afraid I'll get tongue-tied once I open my mouth.

I just hate having all those eyes on me. I've never liked to be the center of attention.

Some of these comments have to do with social anxiety—the fear of doing the wrong thing and feeling embarrassed in a social situation. Social anxiety is nothing to be ashamed of. Most people experience it at some point or another, but some people feel it especially intensely. When social anxiety gets the better of you, just know that you're not alone, and give yourself small little pushes through your fear—for example, by raising your hand to answer a question you're certain of. The more often you do this, and the more often you score small "wins," the easier it will become over time—even if that seems impossible right now. (If this issue is impacting you on a daily basis, though, or if it's inhibiting you from doing things you'd like to do, consider seeking the guidance of a counselor or psychologist.)

At the same time, the more comfortable you get speaking up, the more you'll realize that you don't have to be right or "perfect" in order to merit other people's attention. Some of the comments above have to do with perfectionism, which many introverts suffer from and which is a double-edged sword: It keeps your work at a high quality, but often prevents you from getting your ideas out there at all, since pretty much nothing anyone does or says is ever perfect.

But keeping quiet isn't always about fear, anxiety, or perfectionism. Many introverts simply prefer to wait until we have something meaningful to say (and many I spoke to expressed their wish that everyone else would follow the same etiquette!). In contrast to extroverts, who tend to think out loud, we introverts like to think *before* we speak. In fact, our ability to concentrate deeply on a topic is one of our particular gifts. A teacher calling on us unexpectedly can make us freeze up, since we haven't had time to think through our response. Often, we introverts place so much value on the content and clarity of our answers that we'd rather be silent than simply blurt something out. Sometimes, by the time we think of the thing we truly want to say, the discussion is already over.

Regardless of your reasons for keeping quiet, the students interviewed for this book have come up with many different strategies for making their voices heard. And many said that the more they participate, the easier it gets.

The first step is to find a means of contributing that makes you comfortable. Sometimes this might be as simple as choosing the right seat. One student we spoke with always tried to sit in the front row. That way, when he spoke, he couldn't see the other students turning to face him, and that eased his pressure. Another said he liked sitting near his friends, who made him feel more positive. Still others said that they learned to focus on and direct their comments to the classmates who seem warm and supportive, not the ones who appear too cool and haughty.

Other students focus on how nervous *other* people are. Lola, a sixteen-year-old from Queens, New York, has noticed that her classmates are usually so wrapped up in managing their own social image that they don't notice how nervous *she* sounds. The truth is, sharing thoughts and ideas makes anyone feel vulnerable. Even people who appear confident worry about getting the answer right. In a way, we're all in this together.

Some students have found that speaking in class is easier for them than normal social chitchat. For Liam, a sixth grader from Toronto, Ontario, the classroom setting allows him to express his ideas without getting caught in the back and forth. After he speaks, he explains, his teacher calls on the next person. Liam doesn't have to worry about keeping up, the way he feels he must in conversations with friends.

Grace, the girl we met at the beginning of this chapter, waited to contribute until she'd had time to "warm up." That's what worked for her. But the opposite strategy—preparing in advance to be one of the first to speak—might also suit you. It worked for me, back when I was a law school student.

In January 2013, I spoke about my book *Quiet* at an event in Washington, D.C. My old friend Angie joined me onstage for a Q&A. Angie and I had met as students at Harvard Law School, and we'd recently gotten back in touch. To kick off the evening, Angie told the crowd that when we were in school, she'd had no idea that I was so introverted.

Everyone was surprised, including me. But Angie pointed out that I was always one of the first people to raise my hand in class. How could I possibly have been an introvert?

Her confusion made sense. At Harvard Law School, classes are taught in huge, amphitheater-style auditoriums, in a teaching style known as the Socratic method. The professor randomly calls on the students, and when you're called, you *don't* say no. It's intimidating, but if you signed up for the class, you have to say something. I knew the rules, but I still didn't want to be called on unexpectedly. So I always prepared a few ideas before each class, based on what we'd been studying. Then I'd screw up my courage, raise my hand, and offer my contribution as early as possible, before the discussion veered off into uncharted territory. This way, the professors were less likely to call on me later in the class, at a point where I might not have been ready with an answer. Instead, I knew, they would look for the students who hadn't contributed yet.

This strategy turned out to have another unexpected advantage, documented by social psychologists: The ideas of people who speak up first in a group tend to carry the most weight. So I often found my professors referring back to my contributions throughout the class, making me feel—quite unexpectedly— like a real presence in the room.

I'm not the only one to use this sort of trick, of course. For example, when Davis was in middle school, he couldn't even think about speaking up in a class full of students. Then he received his first B on a report card. His English teacher explained that participation was part of his grade, and since

Davis never raised his hand, he couldn't earn an A, no matter how well he did on his written exams. "It was pick your poison," Davis recalled. "Either get a B, or raise your hand." Davis took too much pride in his work to settle for a lower mark, so he forced himself to raise his hand and read aloud. "I was so scared at first. You're scared that you're going to fumble or trip over your words. I could feel the sweat coming off my forehead. But I would not allow my hand to come down," he said. By taking these kinds of bold steps, Davis came a long way from this fear, as you'll see in later chapters.

For some of you reading this book, it may feel as if your discomfort with speaking in class is insurmountable. But *you can do this*—and you may find that it's much easier than you think. Liam, the sixth grader from Toronto, says he's grown so comfortable speaking in class that he has even started to look forward to it!

Trust me—that can happen for you too.

QUIET SOLUTIONS

It's okay if your heart is beating fast when you raise your hand. Many people feel this way, and speaking up is still worth it. If you don't have time to read through the chapter above, here's a quick list of strategies to ease the process:

STRIKE EARLY: If you know the topic of discussion beforehand, plan out what you're going to say. Develop an opinion or idea, and contribute *before* the discussion rambles off in an unexpected direction.

IDENTIFY YOUR BEST ENTRY POINT: When are you most comfortable pitching in? Develop a strategy for joining the discussion in the way that's easiest for you. Instead of being the first to speak, maybe you prefer building on or adding to another student's comment. Maybe you like to be the person who asks thoughtful questions, or to play devil's advocate. Choose a role that feels natural for you.

USE NOTES: If you're worried about freezing up while speaking, jot down your ideas on a piece of paper so that you can refer to them if needed.

FOLLOW UP: If you had a point to make, but couldn't summon the courage to raise your hand, e-mail your teacher after class, so that she or he knows you're paying attention and are curious.

OBSERVE YOUR CLASSMATES: Notice all the times when other people make nonsensical comments, or say something that's just plain wrong, and no one minds. Develop a warm and forgiving attitude about other people's mistakes, and thus about your own. You'll come to realize that nothing terrible will happen if your answer is wrong or if your voice quivers slightly. "If your answer is incorrect, the teacher will simply move on to the next person," says one wise teen named Annie.

MOTIVATE: The best way to master school life is to find your personal sources of passion. Think about what goal is important to you. The more you care about a topic, the more comfortable you'll feel speaking up about it.

CLASS PARTICIPATION FOR INTROVERTS

misdirection

mind over matter

shrinking

disappearing

wishful thinking

pre-emptive strike

Chapter Three
GROUP PROJECTS, THE INTROVERTED WAY

Group activities are a mixed bag for introverts. On one hand, working with others can mean less pressure—the spotlight is on everyone instead of just you. On the other hand, the need to be social when working in a group can be draining to those of us who prefer to work autonomously.

Karinah, the sophomore from Brooklyn, groans inwardly when her teacher assigns group work. As someone from a big family who shares a bedroom with her sister, Karinah yearns for privacy and time to herself. One of the perks of class time, she says, is that it's a break from the social parts of school, like the hallway or the cafeteria. It can be a relief to be in a place where you're *supposed* to listen quietly.

It's not that introverts don't have ideas to contribute to a group, because we usually do. It's that we don't always want to say them in front of a bunch of people. Sometimes, the swagger of the outspoken kids doesn't leave enough room for soft-spoken students to get a word in. Olivia, a middle-schooler, prefers being teamed up with the less motivated students in her class. "I like being in groups where the kids don't do anything so I can just do it all myself," she said.

This strategy might be easy to fall back on, but why sell yourself short by working with people who don't challenge you? The truth is that the best groups are composed of a mix of introverts and extroverts. Each type of person offers a different perspective on a problem or challenge, and together we cover more ground. You may find yourself in many different kinds of groups—in chapter 6 we'll talk about socializing at parties and in chapter 10 about playing team sports—but group projects in school are perhaps the most challenging. But once you find a role that highlights your strengths and allows your ideas to shine through, your confidence will blossom. Whether you're loud or quiet in groups, this chapter can help you find a role that works for you.

THE RISE OF THE CLUSTERS

I visited dozens of schools while researching my first book and TED Talk, and I was amazed by how many teachers nowadays assign constant group work. In classrooms across the country, desks are pushed together in clusters of four or five, and students are expected to collaborate.

Take Brianna's school in Colorado. Her Spanish class was given a group assignment with lots of creative freedom: Each group would make a video about furniture narrated in Spanish and using vocabulary they had recently learned. Brianna came up with an idea for her group: They could write a script, divide the roles into narrator, director, and editor, and then go to a furniture store like IKEA to shoot the video together.

She thought her approach was sensible, but her five teammates were too busy arguing to listen. They struggled to work together. Each member of the group stood by his or her own idea, and no one seemed interested in hearing anyone else's. So they decided to split up and film their own pieces, then splice them together into one video. "It was really choppy," Brianna said. "Some people did more work than others. I did about half the editing because I wouldn't speak up and say, 'No, *you* have to do this too.'"

Brianna wished she'd been more assertive. "It's kind of easy for a quiet person to be walked on . . . A lot of people take advantage of that," she said. If she could have started the project over, she would have fought harder for her initial plan. She wished that she'd slowed the pace of that first discussion so that everyone in her group had explained what they wanted to do and why. Together, they could have weeded out the ideas that didn't work, and figured out which ones did. Suggesting this would have taken courage, Brianna admitted, but it also would have led to a better final product.

And this kind of courage is more accessible to you than you might think.

T-SHIRTS AND QUIET LEADERS

Although we often hang back in group situations, evidence proves that introverts make strong leaders—often delivering better outcomes than extroverted leaders do. Yes, you read that right—not just decent outcomes, but better ones. Adam Grant, a psychologist at the Wharton School, worked with his colleagues to test the different ways that introverts and extroverts behave in group situations. They recruited 163 college students to participate in their experiment and split them up into teams of five. Each team had one designated leader and four followers. They were then given a pile of T-shirts and a simple task: to fold as many shirts as possible in ten minutes.

Grant's experiment had a twist, though. One "student" in each group was actually an actor who had been taught a really fast, efficient way to fold shirts. At the start of the competition, this actor told his team that he knew a great folding method, and asked if they wanted to learn it. When the leader of the group had a more introverted style, that team was more likely to listen to the actor's idea. The leaders who were more extroverted were less likely to accept input. And this made a big difference. Groups that listened to the tip ended up folding faster.

These findings weren't just about T-shirts, though. Professor Grant also examined the earnings at a chain of pizza shops, and found that the best-performing stores were the ones staffed by proactive employees led by an introverted boss.

Another famous study by Jim Collins found that every single one of the eleven best performing companies in the U.S. were led by CEOs who were described by their peers as "modest," "unassuming," "soft-spoken," "quiet," and "shy." This isn't as surprising as you'd think. Introverts tend to assume leadership positions within groups when they really have something to contribute. Then, once they're there, they listen carefully to the ideas of the people they lead. All of this gives them a big advantage over leaders who rise to the top simply because they're comfortable talking a lot or being in control.

Just take a look at Karinah's story.

Karinah's tenth-grade English teacher divided the class into groups and asked them to make PowerPoint presentations on a historical fiction novel. By the time the presentation was assigned, Karinah had already read the book and understood it well. To call her a bookworm is an understatement; she practically devours her school's reading list, in addition to enjoying fantasy and sci-fi novels on her own. Nonetheless, she was resistant to speaking up about it and wasn't looking forward to being grouped with her peers.

When her teacher assigned the groups, Karinah was surprised to find herself with three students just as introverted as she was. Their first meeting had a lot of pauses. It seemed as if everyone was waiting for someone else to step up as leader. Finally, Karinah found the courage to speak—after all, she'd read the book and had opinions about how imagery and setting were used in the story. "After I shared my thoughts, I asked my group, 'What do you want to do? Does this work for you?'" It turned out that by encouraging other students to speak instead of hogging the spotlight, Karinah helped her team members open up too. Soon, each member put forth an idea of his or her own. "When we were listening to each other, it felt like we had each other's backs," she said.

Having proved to herself that she can speak up in a group and feel listened to, Karinah now feels less anxious when sitting in a cluster of desks. "I've never been able to be the leader before. I think it went well. It turned out that together we actually knew what we were doing. And," she added with a smile, "it felt good to realize that *I* was doing something."

Liam, the sixth grader from Toronto, has also found a way to make group activities work for him—by getting his teachers to agree that the students can choose their own partners. Liam can then work with friends whose skills and knowledge complement one another. For example, his class was assigned the group project of making posters about climate change. Liam and his best friend, Elliot, and their friend Meredith decided to make an electronic poster using Photoshop about the four seasons. "Elliot had ideas about making the poster look good with pictures and bullet points. Our friend Meredith is really smart and knows a lot about science. I know more about Photoshop and computers, so I think altogether we'll have a great project." By choosing a congenial group with a variety of talents, Elliot, Liam, and Meredith created something they were truly proud of.

THE OBSERVANT EDITOR

The ability to listen to others may not sound like our cultural model of strong leadership—but the power of really hearing other people should not be discounted.

Here's how Lucy, a quiet British teenager, used this power to find her own niche as a leader.

As Lucy transitioned from middle school to high school, she began recognizing her unique skills and strengths as an introvert, and embracing her quiet nature. She joined the school magazine, and soon enough was named deputy editor. Among her duties were proofreading, assisting in choosing which articles to publish, and making sure her classmates met all of their deadlines. Lucy could accomplish most of her work in solitude, and when she needed to send a writer feedback on an article, or remind students of their approaching deadlines, she could do so via e-mail. This arrangement suited her temperament.

There were brainstorming meetings with other editors too, but they were all friends, so Lucy felt comfortable contributing. It was at the magazine-wide meetings that she became quiet. During these meetings, all the writers, photographers, editors, and designers met around a table to make announcements; it was an intimidatingly large group compared to her small meetings with the editors.

Even though Lucy didn't speak much, she was far from detached. As we've said, introverts are often great observers, and Lucy is no exception. In addition to listening closely, she watched everyone, studying their reactions. During one early planning session, she noticed a conflict of interest. The staff had unanimously agreed that the first issue should have the collage-y look of a scrapbook or Tumblr page, but when the graphic designer presented her work at the meeting, Lucy saw right away that it hadn't achieved that artsy feel—there weren't enough pictures and the font was too formal. In the meeting everyone said that it looked great, but as Lucy looked around the room, she could tell from the other students' faces that they didn't really mean it. They were either afraid to speak up, or too nice to be critical.

After the meeting, Lucy approached the executive editor to discuss the situation, and she discovered that her intuition was spot-on—the staff was unhappy with the way the design had turned out, but no one knew how to speak up without upsetting the designer. So Lucy came up with a plan: She and the executive editor would meet privately with the designer in order to provide constructive feedback; they would gently suggest taking the design in another direction. In the end, the designer accepted their ideas, and the magazine's first cover was a huge hit with teachers and students.

THRIVING WITHIN A GROUP

I still prefer working alone—it's part of my job as a writer, after all—but even I believe that working with others in a group is an essential life skill. And working in groups is an increasingly large part of my life now that we've launched the Quiet Revolution!

Over the years, I've taught myself how to succeed in group environments. I want you to find the same success—and even comfort. Here are a few tips to guide you along the way:

QUIET, NOT SILENT: You don't need to talk over anyone, or to speak up at every opportunity, but do share your thoughts in a way that's comfortable for you. Perhaps you'll opt for one-on-one conversations with key members of your group. (It can be especially effective to have these conversations before the meeting starts.) Or try written communication as an alternative to speaking in front of a bunch of people: Start a group e-mail or message chain so that you can lay out your thoughts *with-*

out the pressure of wording everything perfectly on the spot. Some teachers may create an online forum for students to discuss ideas, give feedback, or post their results. (If yours hasn't done so, think about suggesting it.)

THE RIGHT ROLE: Lucy found that she contributed best by taking notes, conducting research, and tapping into her powers as an observer. Others are more comfortable playing the role of devil's advocate, or facilitating a group meeting by asking for others' ideas, without necessarily advancing their own. Put time into finding the role or roles that best fit your personality. Behind-the-scenes work is just as important as what goes on in the spotlight—just look at the film and technology industries!

NEW PARTNERS: If you notice that you work well and feel comfortable with certain people, try collaborating with them. That's not to say you should only work with friends or people who are just like you. Test out different partnerships—it can be a good way to get to know new people, and you might find that some classmates bring out your assertive leadership side.

ADVOCATE FOR QUIET: Before any group discussion, suggest that everyone take a few minutes to come up with ideas quietly. This may help both the introverted *and* extroverted members of your group pause and frame their thoughts, leading to more meaningful conversations.

FIND COMMUNITIES OUTSIDE OF SCHOOL: Practice your ability to work in groups by taking extracurricular courses or workshops in subjects or activities you love. Volunteering is also a great way to get involved in projects or groups that speak to you.

TRY "BRAINWRITING": This is a time-honored system in which each member of a group writes an idea down on a Post-it or piece of paper. Then each person puts his or her paper up on a board for everyone to discuss at once. This simple technique makes it easier for everyone to suggest ideas without fear of being interrupted or disapproved of.

HOW TO AVOID BEING INTERRUPTED: If you feel that you tend to be talked over, try this technique. Signal that you want to keep talking by raising your voice slightly and holding up your hand with your palm facing out. This is a polite method that still succeeds in saying, "Back off, I'm not done yet."

SPEAK UP EARLY: Give yourself a little push to speak

up early in a group session. Once you've spoken, you'll feel more comfortable, and others will start directing their own comments to you. You'll feel more a part of things, and this will help you gain confidence.

Chapter Four
QUIET LEADERS

Every year at Grace's school, a select group of twenty-five eighth graders are chosen to help younger students adjust to middle school. They're called "peer leaders." Grace's older sister had been one. She had gushed about what an amazing and motivating experience it was to help the younger kids. In sixth grade, Grace herself had been too shy to make new friends. She wished someone had given her guidance, and now she believed that she could be there for some of the new sixth graders. She thought she could spot those introverted kids and give them a hand as they came out of their shells. She decided to follow in her sister's footsteps and apply.

It was intimidating, but after filling out the necessary paperwork, Grace felt up to the challenge. Applicants were divided into groups of eight for group interviews. Based on the students' performances, the teachers and administrators would select the next crop of peer leaders. Grace knew that she was up against a lot of other kids in her grade: Almost four out of every five kids wanted to be a peer leader. She figured that most of the people chosen would be the talkative, outgoing ones. When the time for her session arrived, she waited outside the school conference room with the other kids. As she suspected, all but one, a soft-spoken boy she knew from class, were what Grace referred to as "screaming extroverts."

Inside the room, two teachers and the vice principal sat at one end of a long table. The kids took their seats, ready to answer interview questions, which were written out on index cards. A few of the kids volunteered immediately, but Grace wasn't ready right away. She understood that she didn't need to be the first to speak. She'd learned from her experience in English class that she was more comfortable going after others. "I wanted to listen and pay attention," she said. "The kids were all jumping in, but I would answer when it was quiet, when no one else was talking, or at the end, when everyone was done."

As Grace grew more comfortable, and began adding her own thoughts to the discussion, she noticed that the quiet boy from her class was saying nothing at all. It seemed as if he was going to offer an answer a few times, but then someone else would start talking. Grace was tempted to tell the others to calm down and give him a chance, but that wasn't her way. Instead, she raised her hand during a lull in the conversation and asked him if he wanted to speak.

"Yes," he replied, "but I was nervous."

To help him out, Grace volunteered the question on her own index card, which asked what he might have done differently if he were starting middle school all over again. The boy answered, and then Grace pitched in with her own response, confessing that she would have tried to branch out more and meet more people, instead of staying within her close-knit group of three girls.

When the interview session was over, Grace wasn't sure how she had fared. Had she spoken enough to show the teachers that she could be a "leader"? A few days later, though, she learned that she'd been selected. And that wasn't the only good news. Thanks to her efforts, the quiet boy in her interview group was named a peer leader too. By helping her peer, Grace had shown true leadership.

WHAT IS A LEADER?

When I traveled around the U.S. visiting different private and public schools, I noticed two problematic trends: The first was that many educators seemed to value leadership as a quality that *all* students should have—even though many students prefer to live autonomously, to chart their own paths. The second was that leadership, whether consciously or not, was usually defined as being extroverted. The young people with so-called leadership skills were usually the outspoken kids. When the quiet kids sought leadership roles in group projects or on the student council, they were often put in charge of secondary work, such as taking notes at meetings or assisting others.

But leadership doesn't require being highly social or attention-seeking. I believe that the time has come to focus on the power of the quiet leader. The most effective leaders are not motivated by a desire to control events or to be in the spotlight. They are motivated by the desire to advance ideas and new ways of looking at the world, or to improve the situation of a group of people. These motivations belong to introverts and extroverts alike. You can achieve these same goals—you can be inspiring and motivational—without compromising your quiet ways.

In sports, business, and the classroom, there are so many different styles of leadership. The brash, bold, popular kids often get the most attention, but don't let appearances fool you! Quiet leaders have risen to some of the highest positions of power in the world. Consider Eileen Fisher, the shy, introverted, and mega-successful clothing designer and company owner. Fisher's introversion inspires her creative work—she says that she learned to design comfortable clothes that would make her feel more comfortable in her own skin.

As an introverted leader, Fisher is in esteemed company. Bill Gates, the genius who transformed Microsoft into one of the most profitable and powerful companies in the world and has since launched the Gates Foundation—one of the world's most innovative philanthropic organizations—is another self-professed introvert. (He even named my TED Talk one of his favorite talks ever!) Another notable introvert is Warren Buffett, the billionaire investor, who is respected as a quiet,

deep thinker who is known for working well with others—
and also for sitting at his desk for hours at a time, poring over
financial documents. Even Martha Minow, the dean of my old
law school, the place where spoken participation is essential,
says she's a strong introvert.

A HUMAN RIGHTS LEADER

One of the most inspiring and enduring examples of an introverted leader in American history is Eleanor Roosevelt. Roosevelt grew up as a painfully shy and careful child, ashamed
of her appearance and of her quiet temperament. Her
mother, a beautiful, social aristocrat, had nicknamed Eleanor
"Granny" because of her demeanor. When Eleanor married an
up-and-coming politician, Franklin Delano Roosevelt, a distant
cousin of hers, his family and friends made it clear that Eleanor
wasn't the light, witty type Franklin had been expected to wed.
Just the opposite: Eleanor was slow to laugh, bored by small
talk, serious-minded, shy. And she was fiercely intelligent.

In 1921, FDR contracted polio. It was a terrible blow, but
Eleanor kept his contacts with the Democratic Party alive
while he recovered, even agreeing to address a party fund-
raiser. She was terrified of public speaking, and not much good
at it—she had a high-pitched voice and laughed nervously at
all the wrong times. But she trained for the event and made
her way through the speech.

After that, Eleanor was still unsure of herself, but she began working to fix the social problems she saw all around her. She became a champion of civil rights, women's rights, and immigrants' rights. By 1928, when FDR was elected governor of New York, she was the director of the Bureau of Women's Activities for the Democratic Party and one of the most influential people in American politics.

FDR was elected president in 1933. It was the height of the Great Depression, and Eleanor traveled the country, meeting with people to discuss their hard-luck stories. When she returned home from her meetings, she often told Franklin what she'd seen, and pressed him to create change. She helped put together government programs for half-starved coal miners in Appalachia. She urged FDR to include women and African Americans in his programs that were putting people back to work.

The shy young woman who'd been terrified of public speaking grew to love public life. Eleanor Roosevelt became the first First Lady to hold a press conference, address a national convention, write a newspaper column, and appear on talk radio. Later in her career she served as a U.S. delegate to the United Nations, where she used her unusual brand of political skills and firmness to help win passage of the Universal Declaration of Human Rights.

She never did outgrow her quiet vulnerability; all her life she suffered dark "Griselda moods," as she called them (named for a princess in a medieval legend who withdrew into silence), and she struggled to develop skin "as tough as rhinoceros hide." "I think people who are shy remain shy always, but they learn how to overcome it," she said. But it was this sensitivity that made it easy for her to relate to oppressed people, and to advocate on their behalf.

CLASS PRESIDENT

Davis, the shy guy we first met in chapter 1, followed in the footsteps of these quiet leaders. Though he felt overwhelmed when he started middle school, he found a way to balance being around his peers and being alone. When solitude wore on him, he joined the middle-school math team and, thanks to his ability to focus intently on problems for a long time, excelled in competitions. Patience was one of his strengths. As he built friendships with other kids on the team, he became more comfortable opening up and sharing his ideas about how the group could work together and improve.

By the time Davis reached eighth grade, he was one of the captains. It surprised him to find that being a leader inspired him—and that he was good at it. An upside to being introverted, Davis found, was being a skilled observer. It meant that he could notice and empathize with what others were feeling, or try to understand where they were coming from. As he began noticing changes that needed to be made within the school as a whole, he decided that *he* wanted to be the one to make the changes happen. So when his homeroom teacher asked for a volunteer to serve on the student council, Davis took a deep breath and did what he usually avoided in class. He raised his hand.

At the first meeting, it was obvious that most of the other kids on the student council were popular. Laughing and chatting around the table, they seemed completely at ease within the group.

Davis wondered whether he'd made a mistake. The only person he knew in the room was his cousin Jessica, a seventh grader who was a lively member of the cheerleading squad.

Jessica knew Davis better than anyone else at school did. Their families had dinner together every weekend. She knew that even though her cousin was quiet and shy, he didn't want to remain in the background. Deep down, he wanted to make a difference—and she believed in his ability to do it. So, when it came time for the election of student body president, she asked her cousin to run. Davis thought she was insane. The most popular girl in school was already planning to run; her victory was almost guaranteed. As one of the only people of color at his predominantly white school, Davis had often been made to feel like an outsider. As he reflected on the student council election, it seemed so uncertain whether people would vote for him—a shy, Vietnamese American guy.

Jessica heard him out, but urged him to trust her. The worst that could happen, she said, was that he'd lose and everyone would forget he ran in the first place. Davis eventually agreed, and as he started planning what he'd do if he were president, his cousin also went to work. She helped him put up posters all around school.

"Everyone was like, 'Who *is* this guy?'" Davis recalled. "They knew I was the nerd, but they didn't know much else."

Before the election, the two candidates delivered short speeches to each homeroom class. Davis was terrified of standing up and speaking. Jessica accompanied him, though, and reminded him that he knew what he was doing. Davis's opponent seemed comfortable at the front of the room. Her platform was quite simple: She promised more social events, like school dances and talent shows. Davis's ideas for the school were more specific. After all, he had spent the last two years observing his school and noticing things that could be improved. His speech was devoted to all of the ways he planned to make changes if he were elected president.

The cafeteria was one of his major issues. The school rules stated that you had to sit with your homeroom; switching tables to sit with friends in other grades or classes was forbidden. Davis had noticed how frustrating this was for most people, and he proposed that as president, he would encourage the principal to let kids sit wherever they wanted, as long as they behaved.

He had also noticed that kids tended to ask each other academic questions before bringing them to their teachers, so he proposed a peer-to-peer tutoring system that would allow kids to exchange knowledge. He shared other ideas as well. Davis was scared as he moved from class to class, but he delivered his message. And his classmates listened.

By the end of the homeroom speeches, both Davis and his opponent had done a good job. She was charismatic and captured the audience's attention. The more she and Davis each spoke in front of the crowd, though, the clearer it was that Davis's ideas were better developed and likelier to succeed.

The results of the election were announced on a Friday morning. The quiet kid who rode home from his first day of school with gum in his hair was the new student body president!

Davis triumphed because he learned to draw on his own natural strengths. He concentrated on substance, not style. Instead of trying to be as social as the most popular kid in school, he focused on being a great candidate. He addressed hard-hitting issues—the things that he noticed as a natural observer. He didn't let his discomfort stop him. He was brave to put himself forward like that—and everyone saw it.

LEADERS AS LISTENERS

As a teenager, I was never a so-called natural leader, but I wasn't a follower, either. Even though I was shy, I had a fiercely determined sense of my own path through the world. Writing was already my passion, so I could have tried to become editor of the school newspaper—but the paper had an enormous staff. I couldn't imagine myself managing that many people. Besides, what I really loved was creative writing, not journalism. So I became the editor of the school's literary magazine, a smaller, more personal publication. The kids who wrote for the magazine were more artistic and unconventional than the journalism crowd; I felt comfortable with them. And among this collection of quirky kids, I learned that I could get things done in my own quiet way. People were open to listening to me and making room for my ideas and my leadership style. One wrote in my yearbook at the end of the year how much he'd appreciated having had a leader he could respect. His words stunned me—it was the first time I ever thought of myself as a leader.

Laurie, an athletic and ambitious teenager from Westchester, New York, described how she cultivated a similarly quiet manner of leadership. Laurie is a classic introvert. When her parents took her to baseball games at Yankee Stadium, she'd tune out the tens of thousands of cheering fans and flip open a novel. No matter how hard she tried to psych herself up for group activities, she couldn't get into the excitement. This side of her personality felt like a flaw; she was ashamed of herself and wanted to create an identity that was more outgoing and social. "I didn't want to say that I was introverted," she recalled. "I felt like it was a negative word."

Laurie thought of herself as other things besides an introvert, though. She also believed she was a leader. In her heart, she knew that these two identities were not contradictory. As a junior in high school, she decided that it was her turn to be a team captain of her track team. Becoming captain was a process: Each student who tried out for the role would interview with the coaches and share her perspective on how to improve the team.

Laurie had already been observing the team for two years, considering exactly that question. When she met with her coaches, she offered a few different ideas. She had noticed that the team could use more unity. There were eighty girls, and some never interacted at all, since their events were so different, from long-distance running to pole vaulting. Laurie wondered whether her teammates would perform better at meets if they felt more support from one another. So, one of Laurie's first proposals was that the girls stretch together as a team at the start of each practice. She also proposed that they perform core or abdominal exercises as a group, since that was something everyone needed to do anyway. And even though Laurie herself was more inclined to small, intimate social gatherings, she suggested that some team dinners, group community service projects, and social outings beyond the track would bring the girls together.

Laurie's ideas made sense to the coaches, who could tell that she'd been paying careful attention. They selected her as one of the captains, and she remained in that role until she graduated. She didn't try to change her personality and force herself to be a loud, outspoken leader. She led by example, first and foremost. In addition to guiding her teammates through the group stretches, she regularly posted team goals on their Facebook page. She wanted the athletes to earn personal bests. The team was good and she encouraged them to strive for a championship.

Laurie was never one to lead the team cheers; it wasn't her thing. She left that to her co-captains. Meanwhile, she connected with her teammates, especially the younger ones, on an individual basis. She'd chat with them before and after practices, answering questions or reviewing what they'd done that day. The more she learned about these girls and what drove them, the easier it was to help them succeed. Before meets, Laurie and her co-captains would gather the team to exchange strategies, everything from how much sleep to get the night before a race to what kinds of food would give them more energy. If the individual members succeeded, the team succeeded. If the team succeeded—then she as a leader had too.

Although Laurie wasn't the loudest, she found that when she did speak, her teammates listened. "As you get closer, and spend more time together, people just naturally start to respect you more as a captain and a leader. And then when you do have to lead practices, people listen to you. They watch what you're doing. You don't need to command their attention by yelling and shouting."

Her teammates appreciated the benefits of her more reserved, personal style of leadership, and Laurie was captain for four seasons. As a senior, she fully saw the effects of her efforts when the team had an unprecedented run of success. "The track program really took off," she said. "We broke a lot of school records and won our league championships twice. Kids were getting into college for track for the first time." Including Laurie, who would go on to run track at Harvard. It was clear that the team owed its success partly to the quiet captain who made room for everyone's voice to be heard.

LEADING WITHOUT SHOUTING

Quietly powerful leaders have guided us throughout history. And as Davis's story exemplifies, your own quiet strength will shine through, even among your louder and bubblier peers. As you read the tips below, keep in mind the words of Sir Winston Churchill, who was prime minister of Great Britain throughout World War II: "Courage is what it takes to stand up and speak; courage is also what it takes to sit down and listen."

Are you seeking a leadership role of your own? Here's a collection of advice to start you on your way:

PLAY TO YOUR STRENGTHS: Davis was terrified when he had to speak in front of his peers, but instead of trying to be the funny, social guy, he focused his speeches on the substantive reasons he was running for office. In the end, his classmates valued

the content of his speeches—and his courage—
more than the smiles of his competitor.

FOLLOW YOUR PASSIONS: Leading people is hard enough,
but trying to do so in the service of a cause or goal
that means little to you is nearly impossible. Whether
it's a charitable cause or a sports team, tap into your
passion, and let others see how much you care.

CONNECT AND LISTEN: Introverts specialize in forging
deep personal relationships. We're great listeners.
Both of these traits can transform you into a powerful leader. When people see that you care about
what they're thinking and feeling, they're more
likely to follow you. If you don't think you excel in
large groups or at the podium, build your alliances
slowly and steadily, one empathetic conversation
at a time.

EMPOWER OTHERS: Dictatorial rule rarely works; no
one appreciates being bossed around. Generous
leaders make sure that others have a sense of purpose, by giving them key roles and by soliciting
their opinions and acting on them when they
make sense. As a listener and observer, you'll be
uniquely tuned in to which roles suit which people in your group.

DON'T BE AFRAID TO DESERVE IT: The fact that you're quiet doesn't mean that you're not strong. It doesn't mean people won't follow you. Laurie believed in herself as a leader, so she sought the role of captain, and she proved to her coaches that they were right to select her.

FIND A ROLE MODEL: No matter how many times I assure you that there is such a thing as a quietly powerful leader, it probably won't mean much to you without a flesh-and-blood example of your own. Think of a person in your life—whether someone you know personally, or a famous figure you admire from afar—who is a strong leader and who has a temperament similar to yours. This will show you that it really can be done—and you can even try to mentally "channel" this person when you're feeling unsure of yourself.

LEAD BY EXAMPLE: This is one of the tenets of leadership, and it's an easy one for the quietest introverts to follow. Showing your classmates, teammates, or friends that you're dedicated and diligent can be just as inspiring as a rousing speech.

PART TWO
SOCIALIZING

Chapter Five
QUIET FRIENDSHIP

We all know loud, charming people who can walk into a room full of strangers and step out an hour later with two or three new soul mates. These kids and adults are held up as our social ideal, as if this is the way we're all supposed to be. For many introverts, though, instant conversation simply isn't natural. We usually prefer a few close friendships to a few dozen acquaintances.

School can feel like a fishbowl—it seems like everything you do is on display for others to see, to judge, and maybe even to criticize. Finding friends who make you feel happy and comfortable is not always easy. An Ohio teenager named Gail described her idea of friendship in this way: "I have three good friends and I'm super-close to all of them. I'd tell all of them anything. I have other people I talk to and have fun with, but I'm very specific about who I do call a friend. A friend is someone I would go to about anything. It's someone who would come to me as much as I go to them."

Julian and his best friend, Andre, who goes to another school, share everything. There's nothing awkward between them. Hanging out together one-on-one suits Julian's introverted, low-key temperament. "Sometimes we just stay in and watch dumb YouTube videos, but mostly we just talk about things and give each other advice and it always feels like time flies. I think he's wise, which is maybe a weird thing to say about a young person, but it feels true."

To Julian's surprise, his friendship with Andre has led him to other close friendships. Initially he felt nervous about meeting up with Andre's other friends: What if they didn't like him or didn't think he was talkative enough? It turned out that they had as much in common with him as they did with Andre. "We still keep it pretty small. There are times we put on music and people dance, but it's not like we go to huge dance parties. I just hang out with people who I like. There are times when it's just me and Andre, and there are times when there are ten people."

FALSELY BUBBLY

Lucy, the shy British teenager we met earlier, tried hard to have a bubbly personality. She hung out with a group of girls at school who shared her interests in reading and biology. A few of them were her polar opposites, though, and Lucy sometimes struggled to relate to them. They did everything in a group, from studying to going to parties. Lucy went along, but she preferred the moments when they were hanging out at home, or one-on-one, just talking and daydreaming together. Despite their differences, Lucy felt secure in these friendships. Her introverted side was a welcome mix in the group, as she often steered their conversations in more thoughtful, meaningful directions.

Still, when she was fourteen, Lucy began to feel that she needed more time to herself, so she started retreating to the library at lunch. She'd never defined herself as an introvert, or even known what that word meant, but she was tired of trying to act gregarious. Eating lunch alone was a relief.

One day, though, she was walking from the library back to her classroom when her friends met her in the hallway. There were nine of them in all, and one stepped forward. "We want to talk to you," she said somberly. She led Lucy outside to the schoolyard, where all the girls sat around her in a circle.

"Why are you ignoring us?" her friend asked, point blank. "It's really mean of you to just wander off at lunchtime and not talk to us, and when we go and find you in the library, you're really abrupt. We're your friends. We deserve better."

The words sunk in. Lucy guessed that her friend was probably right about her being short with them. She hated being interrupted while reading, and so she might actually have brushed them off. But she hadn't meant to upset them. And now this pack of nine girls was sitting and staring at her— some of them angrily.

"I just needed some time to myself," she explained. "I'm not ignoring you, and I'm sorry for coming across as rude."

One girl laid out rules that she said Lucy would have to follow if she wanted to stay in their clique. The first was that Lucy would have to spend time with them at lunch. The second was that Lucy had to tell them when she was leaving for the library.

This experience really shook Lucy. She realized that some of these girls weren't genuine friends: If she wasn't falsely bubbly in front of them, they didn't seem to want her around. She had been pretending to be someone else, so it made sense that the girls were confused when she retreated during lunch.

Over time, her relationship with four of the girls faded, but her bonds with five others who stood by her strengthened. A few even started looking out for her in large group discussions. The girls would draw attention to her by announcing, "Lucy has something to say." She no longer had to hide or explain herself. She didn't have to pretend anymore.

FRENEMIES

An introverted dancer named Georgia had an even more upsetting falling-out with girls who were supposed to be her friends. Ever since preschool, she had been told that she needed to speak up more. Those comments stuck with her as she got older. She hadn't thought of herself as shy or quiet, but since her teachers and peers kept pointing it out, she figured it must be an important part of her identity. And not a positive one, either. Was there something wrong with her? she started to wonder. She had plenty of other traits: She was friendly and athletic. Why were people only talking about how quiet she was? Maybe she was missing something.

In sixth grade, she carpooled to school with a group of girls she'd been friends with for years. She had enjoyed their cheerful and silly dynamic, but now that they were in middle school, the conversations had become snarky. Suddenly popularity and being cool were their number one priorities, and this caught Georgia off guard. The girls made comments about how she wasn't into the right music or clothing. When prank calls started coming in, she suspected immediately that they were the culprits. They denied it, but Georgia knew better than to believe them. "They weren't really good friends," Georgia recalled, "but I didn't have anybody else and I didn't want to be by myself."

In addition to their other insults and slights, the girls talked about how she was too quiet. Before school one day, two of them dared her to scream. "I'll scream," one of the girls said. "Why don't you?"

"I don't want to," Georgia said. Why did they need her to scream? It was obviously just to make her uncomfortable!

The two girls then took turns yelling at the top of their lungs. Georgia would not follow along. She tried to look amused, but all she wanted to do was cry.

Unfortunately, this sort of abusive relationship is common in middle school, particularly among girls. This is a generalization and not an out-and-out rule, but often boys work out their differences through physical fights or contests, battling with their fists or on the playing field. Girls more often resort to something called relational aggression. Some girls use their relationships with other girls as weapons to intimidate and belittle these supposed friends, all in the name of power and popularity. The writer Rachel Simmons brilliantly chronicles this epidemic in her book *Odd Girl Out,* citing numerous cases of kids who were hurt deeply by this form of bullying.

Of course, girls aren't the only ones to practice this kind of hostility. In fifth grade, a quiet boy named Raj was thrilled when he was asked to move up to a higher-level math class. He loved math, and the invitation to switch to an accelerated class was a real boost to his confidence. So his parents were shocked when he said he might stay in the regular class.

Later, they discovered that a few boys had warned him that they wouldn't be friends with him anymore if he switched to the accelerated class. At first, Raj didn't want to risk losing those friends. But then, on his own, he came to a different decision. He loved math. He wanted to take the class. And if the boys didn't support him, that meant they weren't really his friends. Taking that class was more of a confidence boost than hanging out with those so-called friends.

Relational aggression is particularly powerful when used against quiet kids, both boys and girls. Often, introverted kids worry that they won't be able to make new friends, so they hold on to abusive relationships as long as possible. They often remain in confidence-shattering cliques out of fear of the unknown, reasoning that a bad friend is better than no friend at all.

Thankfully, many young people summon the courage to resist this kind of social pressure. Walking away from mean or bullying friends takes a tremendous amount of guts—but believe me, you are capable of it.

In the end, Georgia found that courage too. At first, she didn't want to lose those girls, and so she sat with them at lunch every day even though they often used the time to make fun of her. At the end of sixth grade, though, she decided it was too much. She'd been stepped on for too long and she wasn't going to let that happen to her ever again. She told her parents she never wanted to carpool with those girls again. She wasn't going to stay in touch with them, either.

The process of making new friends felt impossible. The whole grade seemed as if it had been divided into impenetrable cliques, and now that she'd dropped her supposed friends, Georgia was on her own. Then, in her seventh-grade science class, she was placed in a seat next to a girl named Sheila. They didn't know each other very well, and they didn't talk much at first. But one day Sheila started laughing at something the teacher had said, and for some reason Georgia started laughing too. Soon neither of them could stop. The teacher had to tell them to be quiet, and Georgia was secretly thrilled. It was the first time she'd ever heard *that* from a teacher!

After that day, the two girls started talking more, laughing at each other's doodles in class, and working on their lab assignments together. Through Sheila, Georgia started becoming friendly with another girl as well. The three girls played basketball and tennis together. They had silly conversations and also serious ones, talking about what they wanted to do when they grew up, and how they hoped to help people and truly make a difference in the world.

"They weren't as 'popular' as my former group had been," says Georgia, "but I realized that image wasn't everything and that popularity didn't really matter. I felt not only accepted for who I was but also appreciated. I had made genuine friends."

Eighth grade was even better. Georgia solidified her bond with her new friends, and grew closer to other girls as well. As she grew older, she started to redefine her idea of friendship.

one close
friendship

=

a bunch of
acquaintances

She realized that her quiet side didn't have to be a drag on her ability to form those bonds. In fact, she found that from the tennis courts to the dance hall, the opposite proved true. "Being quiet was a strength because I was able to build a few close friendships rather than a bunch of superficial ones," she said. "I was able to share my feelings and thoughts and connect with my friends on a deeper level."

JUST A HELLO

If you're struggling to make friends, that's okay: It takes time to make the right ones, the kind who will support and value you. Hailey from Michigan was so shy that she often struggled just to say hello. In fourth grade, she decided that she was going to stretch herself to greet more people. Just a quick hello—she didn't even need to start a full conversation.

And yet this small act of willpower brought some amazing results. One of the first people Hailey forced herself to say hi to was a new girl who had just moved into town. "I went up and said hello to her, and we started talking, and we found out we had a lot of stuff in common," she recalled. The girl appreciated Hailey's gesture. "It made her feel more welcome because not a lot of people had come up and said hello to her." Five years later, the two girls were still friends, and rooming together at a boarding school nearby.

When Davis graduated from high school, he worried that

he wasn't going to know how to make friends in college. He decided that he needed to come up with an icebreaker. Over the summer, he taught himself some magic tricks. "I thought if I didn't know how to approach people, I could do magic, and that would lead to a conversation," he said. And sure enough, when Davis arrived on campus, he carried his playing cards with him, and introduced himself to new people by asking them to pick a card. Then he'd do a trick and, more often than not, settle into a conversation with the person. "I actually met some of my best friends through that," he said.

These interactions boosted his confidence, and Davis eventually decided that he was using the cards as a crutch for an ailment that no longer existed. The magic tricks were the equivalent of having his outgoing cousin Jessica next to him during that eighth-grade election, prodding him along. By the end of his first year of college, he didn't need them anymore. If he wanted to meet someone, he'd just walk up and introduce himself.

NATURAL LISTENERS

What Hailey and Davis might not have realized is that we introverts have a skill that is especially helpful in making new friends: We are great listeners. Have you ever been stuck in a social situation where you're just not in the mood to talk? I sure have. Small talk can be nerve-racking. I feel like I'm on my toes, trying to come up with the next clever thing to say. On top of that, discussing the weather or gossip doesn't satisfy me. There's nothing wrong with it, but I usually itch for more. That's when I become an interviewer.

A lot of introverts say that when they're feeling withdrawn around others, they get through conversations by deflecting, or pushing attention away from themselves onto other people and things. If I'm feeling especially introverted at a time when I'm supposed to be chatty, I start asking the other person questions about him- or herself. Let chattier people do most of the talking. You'll probably genuinely enjoy listening to their answers. Other people's stories are often more interesting than you'd expect, and you learn much more by listening than by talking.

Of course, you have to be careful not to make the conversation too lopsided—the people you're talking to want to feel heard, not grilled. So don't be afraid to interject your own thoughts and opinions into the mix.

Many journalists say that they found their calling through exactly this process. For Ira Glass, the host of the popular radio show and podcast *This American Life*, a big part of his job is to make conversation with people. In his interviews, he skillfully puts people at ease and draws out their stories, feelings, and beliefs. Yet Glass says that he's "not a natural storyteller at all. If anything," he told Slate.com in a 2010 interview, "I'm a natural interviewer, a natural listener, but I'm not a natural storyteller."

Glass may do less of the talking, but his ability to listen closely, ask the right questions, and interject interesting observations makes for a fascinating show. The ability to make a person feel comfortable and heard—and in so doing, to reveal fascinating and hidden truths—is just one of an introvert's many superpowers.

USE YOUR WORDS

But sometimes all of this listening can wear on you. You've taken in so much information from other people, but where is *your* voice in the conversation? Don't your thoughts matter just as much? Why shouldn't it be *you* who is listened to?

Have you ever heard parents telling their small children, "Use your words"? I heard a dad say this to his crying child recently. He wanted to help his son, but he couldn't understand why the boy was upset. In between gasps and sobs, the boy wasn't explaining *why* he was crying.

People aren't mind readers. As much as we want someone to understand us implicitly, sometimes we have to provide more information. *We* have to do the talking. Speaking out is sometimes scary, but saying what you want or need is also very empowering, and more often than not you'll be pleased by the response you'll get.

When you're comfortable—or even if you need to stretch a bit—use your words. Share your ideas, thoughts, and feelings.

It's not conceited or boastful to claim attention for yourself. It's also not a betrayal of your introverted self to want to be heard. Friendship is about give *and* take—about making the time to listen patiently and attentively, and about trusting your friend enough to express yourself honestly in return.

FORGING QUIET FRIENDSHIPS

There's no single trick to finding a true, devoted friend. I've suggested a few possibilities here, but the most important thing is to keep your mind and heart open. Your next best friend could be that quiet new kid in the corner, or the loud and popular one standing on the table in the middle of the cafeteria. And you, with your interest in deep one-on-one conversations and willingness to listen closely, can be a valuable friend to them both.

BE YOURSELF: Don't try to be someone you're not, in order to impress. A true friend will appreciate you for you. "Don't fake being an extrovert to gain friends," advises an introvert named Rara. "One good friend is so much better than a lot of acquaintances. Even if that means sometimes you're alone, it's better than having to be fake around people." At the same time, look for the friends who bring out your true self—your silly side, your uninhibited side, your dramatic side. That's how you'll know you're truly "home."

RISK SOLITUDE: Extract yourself from mean groups of people or friendships that feel toxic. As Georgia learned, it's better to have no friends than to stay in a damaging, bullying relationship. You deserve to be around people who make you feel relaxed and yourself—whether you're feeling happy *or* sad.

JOIN A GROUP: This advice may sound counterintuitive to a quiet person. But a team, club, or extracurricular activity can be a great way to build new friendships. This is especially true if the group is organized around a topic that truly interests and even excites you. You'll spend time with people who share your interest, and there's less pressure to make a great first impression. "When you're joining a class or a group that you're going to attend regularly, you'll be able to make friends more easily," says Jared, an introverted boy from California. "You can get to know each other slowly and let time do the work."

START SMALL: A teenager named Mitchell spent several years moving from place to place as his father, an army officer, was transferred from one military base to another. As a result, Mitchell was forced to develop a strategy for making friends. His rule? Find one good friend first. Once he'd solidified that bond, and found someone he could truly trust, he would start thinking about branching out and building more friendships.

TEAM UP: A teen named Teresa says that she struggles to make new friends on her own, but when she's with one of her outgoing friends, she meets people she might not have otherwise. "I have found the best way to meet new people is by having my friends with me," she says. "It's a great way of being in your comfort zone while socializing."

ASK QUESTIONS: Listening is one of your superpowers, so use it when meeting new people by asking questions about them, and then asking follow-up questions that show you're paying careful attention. You'll learn a lot about the person quickly, and as a bonus, you'll be giving yourself a break from talking while the other person tells you his or her tales. (Just be careful not to turn the conversation into a one-sided interview! People want to hear a little from you too.)

EMPATHIZE: Everybody feels insecure or awkward sometimes—even the most extroverted, charismatic, or intimidating person in the cafeteria. By imagining what others might be feeling, you'll find yourself more comfortable around them.

USE YOUR WORDS: Remember that nobody is a mind reader. Eventually you'll need to speak up to make sure that people know how you're feeling. A true friend will want to listen.

Chapter Six
QUIET PARTIES

When I was in middle school, a few of my friends threw me a surprise birthday party. We spent hours talking, laughing, and listening to music. It was incredibly nice of them to go to all that trouble for me, and I was lucky to have them in my life. But I have a confession. A few times during the evening, I looked around at the half-dozen girls in the room and felt a surge of disappointment. Don't get me wrong; I wasn't disappointed that these girls were my friends. Not at all. But I couldn't help thinking that there should have been more of them. I kept thinking that if one of the other kids in my grade had a surprise birthday party, there would have been seventy or eighty people there. This was supposed to have been a special night, but even after all their efforts, I ended up feeling like a social failure.

I look back on that night now and think what a waste of worrying that was. Some people enjoy a social circle of six, some of sixty, some of six hundred. And it's all fine. This can be hard to believe when you're first discovering how you fit into the social world, but take my word for it—as long as you have friends you enjoy, it doesn't matter how many of them there are. The irony is that if my friends had organized a crowded party with seventy or eighty people jammed into my house, I would've hated it!

Being introverted doesn't mean that you won't enjoy—or be socially skilled at—crazy parties, of course. (I happen to love to dance, and sometimes love a great dance party.) But these environments are more draining for us, for all the reasons we talked about earlier. Full-fledged extroverts draw energy from loud bashes. But since we're more sensitive to stimulation, the lights, faces, voices, and pounding music of a loud party can be unappealing. It's as if all humans have a social battery, but that battery drains and recharges under completely different conditions. I've come to recognize this feeling of my battery draining, so I know when it's time for me to leave a party, or retreat to a couch for a more intimate chat—and a battery recharge.

You can do the same thing. One introverted friend of mine attends pretty much every party she's invited to—and in her quiet way she's very popular, so that's a lot of parties. She enjoys being there and everyone is happy to see her. She also usually leaves after an hour or two, gracefully saying her thanks and good-byes, and moving on her way. No one notices, and no one minds—they're just happy that she was there.

Similarly, when a swimmer named Jenny (whom you'll

hear more about in chapter 10) was younger, she felt the pressure to have a big birthday party like everyone else. But once her friends arrived, she would start taking extra-long trips to the bathroom. She'd shut the door and stay in there to allow herself a chance to settle down. These moments of quiet restored her energy so that she could enjoy herself more when she stepped out into the party again.

You just need to find the system that works for you—and then stop worrying about it.

THE MAGICIAN'S GREATEST TRICK

In fact, there are all kinds of ways to show up that can work for the party-shy.

Take Carly's experience at junior prom. Prom is always made out to be an epic night of partying. As if dancing all night with her entire grade wasn't overwhelming enough to Carly, there was the added pressure to make it the *"best night ever."*

Junior prom was a big deal at Carly's school. Her grade was divided into a wide variety of cliques. There were the jocks and the cheerleaders, there were the kids who were into hunting, and then there was Carly's group, whom she lovingly referred to as the "artsy weirdos." Carly, her friends, and their dates decided to keep the night low-key. They met up for a pre-hangout at her house before heading to prom. They took pictures and got take-out food. It was a relief to ease into the night of the big party with the people she cared about most. She had a great time and danced the night away—but she still preferred the night after, when she and her friends cooked dinner together and talked about the party in the comfort of her own kitchen.

Davis, whom you met earlier, was turned off by big parties too, but he figured out a way to deal with those feelings. In middle school, he only attended the big celebrations when required. As class president, he had to attend homecoming, but once his job was done, and the king, queen, and other royals had been announced, his parents picked him up. Davis wasn't antisocial. Just the opposite. But he already understood that he preferred a different kind of gathering. In high school, he was the social ringleader of his group of friends. He would invite everyone over to his house on the weekends instead of joining the mobs at the big parties. They'd hang out playing video games or cards. His house was the hotspot for his buddies.

As he grew older, his preference for these intimate gatherings had an unexpected effect. In college, if someone invited him to a big party, Davis would decline, but he'd quickly suggest something else instead. He would invite the person to meet for coffee the next day or to join him at the art gallery to check out a new exhibit. In doing so, he was making it clear that it was the party that turned him off, not the person. Usually the person accepted his invitation, and these more intimate outings didn't only appeal to other introverts. He found that his more outgoing classmates, the ones who relished the parties he tried to avoid, also enjoyed chilling out one-on-one. It was a refreshing change from the way they usually hung out with their friends.

Davis ended up forging deeper friendships even though he turned down those initial invitations. Avoiding the parties was his choice, and he knew he wasn't hurting anyone's feelings or unintentionally making enemies. Still, he did have a concern. "I was worried that if I didn't go to parties, no one would know who I was."

It's not that Davis sought popularity, exactly. He just didn't want to be anonymous. Soon, though, he found out that his fears were baseless. Near the end of his freshman year of college, he was walking across campus with one of his friends, saying hello to the people he knew. "Hey, Davis," his friend said, "do you realize that you know half the campus?"

"What are you talking about?" Davis asked.

"We just walked down the street and you knew half the people!"

His friend's random observation was confirmed a year later. Davis entered the campus talent competition, hoping to show off a few of his magic tricks. The audience chose the winner. When the contest was over and Davis heard the loudest cheers in his favor, he looked out at the crowd of five hundred. His supporters weren't strangers. They were his friends. And they were true friends, not the kind of acquaintances you just follow on Instagram or nod "hey" to at a party. These were classmates he'd talked to about life and love and everything in between. Looking out at the seats, he realized he was far from anonymous. His good friends filled up half the auditorium.

THE SOCIAL BUTTERFLY AND THE PAINTER

On the outside, Noah, a young filmmaker from Baton Rouge, Louisiana, was always a social butterfly and a great storyteller. He seemed to thrive around people. But after a while, he would grow sharply aware of how much he wanted to slip away from the crowd and be by himself. In middle school, his core friends were gamers like him. They'd all play together, or individually in the same room with one person on an iPad, another on an Xbox, and someone else on his phone. But by ninth grade the social scene was changing—people had started dating, and friendships were up and down. Noah stayed friendly with the guys individually, but the group split up. He started getting involved in extracurriculars, including the school's online newspaper and the a cappella group. He made new friends in each activity, but he never felt like a firm part of anything.

"I was dabbling in lots of groups. That's part of the social butterfly thing: I had good friends, but no best friends. At parties when people were bonding and maybe falling in love with each other, or creating friendships that would last forever, I was always a little uncomfortable. I remember falling asleep lonely when I got home from a party—it was loneliness mixed with hope. Like, in the future, this will get better and I'll find my place."

There's an assumption that everyone else is the well-adjusted, fun-loving version of themselves that they present on social media. Or that middle school and high school are the years of your life when the best parties take place, and when you first fall in love. The truth is, it all happens for everyone at different times. For many people (and I'm raising my own hand here), their best, most socially comfortable years come much later, in college or well beyond. There aren't any rules on how to have the "right" kind of social life at school any more than there are rules on which table in the cafeteria is the "right" one to sit at. You can carve out what works best for you—even if your version of social is different from the models you see in movies and on TV.

Laurie's version wasn't the raging party, either. Huge get-togethers didn't appeal to her, so she started putting together smaller events—painting parties. Her favorite social time was in painting class. With just half a dozen other girls, it was a nice break from the standard crowded, competitive classroom. Most of the artists didn't know one another at the start of the year, but over time they became close. One night, Laurie and one of her good friends from the class decided to get together and paint. Before long, a few of the other girls were joining them for painting parties, and eventually these became a weekly event.

They would get together at around seven and paint until midnight. Sometimes they'd work on their class assignments, but the parties weren't all work. "We played music," Laurie recounted. "We'd eat a lot of food. We had great conversations. Sometimes we'd get sidetracked and not paint, and just eat and talk about life." Over time, the girls in the art class became some of her closest friends.

BE SAFE

If you're really dreading a social event, it's okay to skip it. It happens. Stretching like a rubber band is important, but remember that we all have our limits and need to protect ourselves. Unfortunately, some people get into the habit of depending on substances such as alcohol or marijuana to relax at parties. Peter, an introverted college student from Oberlin, Ohio, would actually use smoking breaks as his way to avoid being around people for a while during a party. If you find that you can't behave a certain way unless you have drugs or alcohol in your system, please talk with a trusted adult. There are much safer ways to find comfort.

Alcohol and pot are downers anyway, which means that the euphoria they create can quickly give way to depression and anxiety. I hate to sound preachy, but here's the truth: Not only are these solutions unhealthy, they're also temporary. The high will wear off and you'll go back to your usual self. The most sustainable solution is to get better and better at being who you already are, and to learn what situations make you the most comfortable and how to find comfort in situations that aren't ideal.

HOW TO PARTY LIKE AN INTROVERT

You can't always design or find your ideal party. Sometimes you're going to be asked to attend the crowded bashes that make you uncomfortable. But there are ways to ease these moments and get the most out of them. Here are a few suggestions:

FIND A WINGMAN/WINGWOMAN: If you're obligated to attend a huge party, start out by attending with someone you know. Arrange to meet this person beforehand, if you can. The transition into the wild, packed room will be much easier if you enter with a friend or two, rather than agreeing to meet them there.

ARRANGE AN OUT: Pick a reasonable goal for yourself—an hour, perhaps—and inform your parent or guardian to be on call at that appointed time. Then, if you find yourself overwhelmed, text them to come and pick you up.

HOW TO LEAVE A PARTY EARLY

secret passageway

puff of smoke

disguise

polite good-bye

flying piñata

START ON THE FRINGES: Once you arrive, give yourself time to adjust to the noise and movement. Linger with your friends around the borders of the room first, where it's likely to be slightly calmer.

CULTIVATE A BUBBLE: At first, try to shrink the space down to your small group of friends, or even to a conversation with just one person. Don't think about what's happening outside your bubble—who's doing or saying what. Focus on your friends and allow yourself to get acclimated before venturing out.

TAKE A REJUVENATING BREAK: When the noise or crowd becomes too much for you, retreat to the bathroom or another quiet area to relax and recharge your battery. Just a few minutes of peace and quiet can do wonders.

STAY A LITTLE BIT LONGER: Every once in a while, try staying an extra half hour past the time when you first want to leave. You might find yourself getting beyond the discomfort, having fun, and talking to people who surprise you.

DO-IT-YOURSELF: When you're hosting your own celebration, don't feel that you have to follow the norm. If you enjoy spending time with a few good friends, then limit your party to that number. A small, intimate party is nothing to be ashamed of. For many people, it's more fun!

INITIATE PLANS THAT WORK FOR YOU: Similarly, if you're sick of getting dragged along to parties or big group hangouts, why not invite people to do something *you* want to do, like get pizza with a few friends, or go on a bike ride around the neighborhood? Your friends will probably be excited about the change of pace.

STAY DRUG-FREE: You don't need to turn to any substances to make yourself artificially comfortable. Trust yourself, avoid dangerous people and situations, and take care of your body.

STAY CURIOUS, STAY COMPASSIONATE: Almost everyone has an interesting story or an interesting view of the world. When you meet someone new and feel that awkward moment of small talk setting in, give yourself a challenge: Your job is to find out what makes this person interesting. Remember too that even the smoothest or most intimidating people carry their own inner pain. This is part of being human. Even if you never find out what each person's individual source of pain is, remembering that it's there will help you cultivate an open and compassionate attitude toward everyone you meet.

Chapter Seven
#QUIET

Picture this: You're bundled up in a cozy sweater, with a delicious snack by your side. Maybe you're curled up with a juicy novel, or streaming the next episode in a marathon viewing of your favorite show. Maybe you're scrolling through hilarious GIFs on Tumblr or about to beat the next level of Final Fantasy. It's Saturday evening and you're excited to spend time on your own. You can't think of anywhere you'd rather be, until . . . *ding!* It's a phone notification. Someone you follow on Instagram has posted a photo of a group of people you know, laughing and in the middle of what looks like a great event.

Your stomach flips. What are they doing? Are they having the time of their lives? If so, will they talk about it on Monday? And why, you wonder, aren't you there? Even though just a moment ago you were happy and comfortable, you're suddenly struck by worry: Is being quiet at home enough when everyone else is out having fun?

This is a classic FOMO moment: Fear of Missing Out. As introverts, we're often naturally drawn to quieter, more intimate settings. We know how beautiful or cool our sanctuaries can be. Yet seeing photos on Facebook of cliques from school at big parties can feel like a reminder of all the socializing we "should" be doing.

Social media can intensify that anxiety about being excluded. Even if having a quiet night is what you'd *rather* do, finding out about other people's Saturday nights online can make you question your lifestyle. Lola, for example, is an introvert who is close friends with her school's popular crowd. Though she loves her friends, she often feels that they expect her to be more social than she is—both in person and online. Her phone stresses her out because it holds texts, Snapchat, Twitter: It's all there waiting for her to observe what others are up to, and urging her to take part.

"If I seclude myself, I feel like I'm missing out. My friends will DM cute guys on Instagram, and I feel kind of jealous of that. But I want to be able to meet people in person. I'm in this weird conflicting thing where I feel like I'm old-fashioned because I love to do fun, quirky stuff face-to-face. I don't know that many other people who feel this way. I want to be part of this and connect with people, and at the same time it makes me kind of unhappy. There's always evidence of other people doing fun stuff."

Now that Lola is starting her senior year of high school, she doesn't have regular FOMO moments anymore. She has decided that she doesn't need to regret having missed something if she was perfectly happy doing what she chose to do instead. In fact, she finds herself using social media as a way to keep in touch with her friends during those times when they've gone in different directions. By texting or Snapchatting with them while they're apart, she feels more looped in and less excluded. In that way, social media actually allows her to feel connected to her friends while sticking to her introverted ways.

And when that old FOMO feeling threatens to pop back up, she has a trick for getting rid of it. "Sometimes when I'm doing things that I want to do for myself, like hang out and listen to music in my room or practice skateboarding, I put my phone on Do Not Disturb so I won't have to worry about feeling like I should be doing something else in that moment."

On the flip side, Colby, an introverted student at a boarding school, has found that social media has actually brought him out of his shell. "I talk to people on Facebook, usually for group chats to plan something. I'll flip through it to check in with people and make a date to hang out." Colby gets invited on Facebook to events that he thinks he probably wouldn't hear about otherwise, and he has met people at these parties who've become his close friends. He likes the fact that he can see who's planning to attend, so he knows if he'll have friends there. Using social media for this purpose has really opened up his social life.

SPACE TO SHARE

Noah also sees benefits to being on Instagram, Snapchat, and so on. He uses social media not just to catch up with friends, but also to post and share the things *he* cares about—especially movies. "I'm over using it to show off the way that you look, or how cool you are. I'm more interested in social media that's about something you're passionate about." Then he jokes: "And obviously cute animal pictures too."

Noah makes a great point. For those of us on the introverted spectrum who are often resistant to being in groups, we may find it easier to explore our interests online—and apps and the Internet are great ways to connect with the world around you. Lola, for example, started posting her collages on Tumblr and was amazed by the response she got. She has since connected to other young, ambitious artists who are also interested in sharing their work. The girls she has met across the country have become her pen pals in a way—trading inspiration online.

Maybe you have a special interest that no one else in your neighborhood or school has, and you want to meet others who can relate to you or teach you about it. Maybe no one else at your school is of the same race or culture, and you want to connect with people who have experience walking in your shoes. Many students told me that when they felt alone in their day-to-day lives, they were relieved to find entire communities of people like themselves online. It gave them the courage to talk openly about things that mattered to them, such as speaking out against racism or bullying.

The Internet, unlike the classroom, is a great place for quiet people to express themselves without having to compete against others for a chance to speak. And social media can be an opportunity to find validation: Many teens told me that when they felt insecure or underappreciated by the people around them, their confidence was boosted by getting likes on Facebook or Instagram. Of course, you don't want your confidence to depend solely on the number of likes or retweets you've gotten, but as Noah said, it feels great to share things about yourself—especially when you feel shy about doing so in person.

Make your circles of friends OVERLAP

WI-FI FRIENDSHIPS

Are quiet people more outgoing online? Do we test out a more extroverted personality on social media? For several years now, psychologists have been trying to figure out whether people act the same way online as they do in real life. In one study, scientists analyzed the Facebook profiles and pages of a group of college students. They found that the extroverts had more wall posts, photos, and friends; they sought out social interactions and engaged more with the crowd. The introverts, on the other hand, were more often watchers. In other words, introverts and extroverts usually behaved like themselves online.

Many introverts I spoke to told me that they didn't post often, but that they often checked in and chatted with friends online. Virtual networks were a way of maintaining or even strengthening their real relationships. In 2012, a group of scientists from the University of California, Irvine, discovered similar trends when they studied how teens use online communication. The scientists questioned 126 high school students about how they engaged with one another through social media, and they found that for most kids, their online and offline friends were one and the same.

Noah is perhaps an exception: He has made new friends online with people all over the world—without ever meeting them face-to-face. "I made some weird and surprising connections with people online on MMORPGs [massively multiplayer online role-playing games] like EverQuest, or World of Warcraft, where you're playing with thousands of people at once, and everyone has an avatar. I was always inspired by the story, or the creative elements of the game, so we would bond over that." For Noah, these friendships were often less stressful than his friendships with classmates, with whom he felt pressure to be fun and cool on the spot.

Befriending people online has its ups and downs. Studies show that these virtual friendships can be positive and empowering, but they can also be a barrier to finding friends IRL, in real life. One fourteen-year-old boy we met was part of a virtual team in a combat game online; his team was made up of boys from across the country. Although he referred to these boys as some of his best friends, they never shared their stories or real-world experiences, and he had no plans to meet any of them in person. In some cases he didn't even know their real names.

Always keep in mind that most people present an airbrushed version of their lives online. Think about what gets posted to Instagram: photos of vacations, or of delicious meals, or of moments at parties when we're mid-laughter and flanked by friends. What about those less glamorous moments eating cereal in pajamas on a Sunday morning? Or more vulnerable moments when we're feeling lonely or nervous? If you only get to know people through their social media presence, you might not see that they feel just as fragile as you do—including the extroverted ones!

The child psychologist Aimee Yermish counsels her patients

to examine their relationships thoughtfully. If a friendship consists mostly of gaming or of an online connection, then it has limitations. That's because the term *friend* is only *partly* represented online. A true, mature bond includes a personal and social connection, of the kind you develop sitting across from someone, chatting over a snack. Yermish tells her patients to approach their digital friendships the same way they approach them offline: Look for people who might become true friends over time. It's helpful to think of digital communities, from Facebook to online gaming, not as complete worlds in and of themselves. Think of them as a way to forge stronger connections in the real world.

Frankly, since the Internet is open to everyone, there are a lot of creeps and criminals out there, and bullies too. Be careful about what you say online and don't be quick to trust a stranger. I won't lecture you on this too much, because hopefully it's something your parents and teachers have talked about, but please make sure you know which pieces of information you should—and shouldn't—be sharing online. And remember that there's always a chance that a photo or video you post will be shared without your consent. Make sure that you aren't texting or Snapchatting a photo that you wouldn't want a stranger—or a classmate—to see. No matter how loud and proud your online persona is, while you're having fun, please make sure you're also staying safe!

IRL

It's tempting to compare your own friend count on Instagram to somebody else's, and I'm sure this would have caused me lots of anxiety when I was a middle-school student. Even without Instagram, Snapchat, and the like, people often feel insecure about the number of friends they have. In one Internet study, scientists interviewed college students and found that those with high friend counts were often happier with their lives. They believed they had more social support because of all their digital friends on Facebook.

The way New Hampshire teen Robby saw it, though, was this: Friend and follower counts are just virtual versions of the popularity contests that have always played out in school. For a kid like him, who values deeper personal connections, those numbers mean nothing. A friend is someone he'd be able to share his failures and disappointments with, not just his triumphs and best jokes.

Many of the quiet kids we heard from shared Robby's views on friend counts, but they still valued communicating on apps and online. When you think about it, it's pretty incredible to have this platform that gives a voice to people who don't always feel comfortable having one. In middle school, Robby himself often felt too wrapped up in his own head, or too nervous about being judged, to toss off jokes in conversation. "When I was younger, if I was in a group of friends and someone said something funny, I'd think of something funny to go on top of that. But I'd think to myself before I spoke, 'Is this the right thing? Would it be weird?' Then it would be too late."

When Robby had enough time to reflect and think of a joke, he could be really funny, so he would craft clever responses to his friends via text or Facebook chat. On one level he felt great about being more extroverted and confident online. "It's so easy when it's just a string of characters on your cell phone display," he recalled. He could show friends what was going on inside his head and reveal a side of himself that he normally struggled to express.

But what Robby really wanted was to crack those jokes in real life, with his friends right there in front of him. So he decided to devote less and less time to social media. "When I was younger, I was taking advantage of Facebook and instant messaging, but if you let yourself use those crutches, then you're putting yourself in a situation where maybe that's all you're capable of," he said. "I don't want people to see me in a way that's not really me, and I don't want to see people in a way that's not really them."

Robby was determined to become that confident, witty person he imitated so easily online. Being part of a band and gaining confidence from playing in front of people was a huge help. But he also counted a job at the supermarket as an important step. The summer before his senior year of high school, he landed a job as a cashier at the local market. The small talk he had to make with customers all day gave him confidence. "I had these insignificant conversations a hundred times a day. Before, I was so incredibly uncomfortable with that, but not anymore." To Robby, this experience was a testament to the power of repetition. "You're not going to become more confident just through willpower. Practice is important."

Still, being a classic introvert, Robby found himself mentally exhausted after these interactions. He needed to retreat to his room and listen to music for a while to unwind—and, of course, to check Facebook.

HOW TO GET THE MOST OUT OF SOCIAL MEDIA

Everyone uses social media differently. You might love it or hate it, and there's no need to be a big part of the online scene if it makes you uncomfortable. For many shy introverts, the Internet is an ideal chance to connect without the pressure of being face-to-face with others. But to some, hanging out with people in real life feels more authentic. Just remember that whoever you are offline is just as great as your online self. Here are a few suggestions for navigating the strange and bewitching world of social media:

RETAIN YOUR PRIVACY: Keep your social media profiles private, so that only you and your friends can see them. Not only is this safer, but it also allows you to experience the Internet on a more comfortable scale. If you prefer smaller groups in the real world, you might want to keep your Instagram and Facebook communities small as well.

VALUE YOUR TRUE FRIENDS: You might be lucky enough to start a real friendship online, but balance this by also maintaining friendships in person. Social media is often a better tool for enhancing your existing friendships than for starting new ones.

EXPRESS YOURSELF: One of the great things about social media is how easy it is to share your thoughts, ideas, or even artwork, photos, and videos with others. Many introverts find it easier to be "heard" online.

FIND YOURSELF: The Internet is incredibly vast and full of materials and communities devoted to every topic imaginable. It's a great resource for exploring your interests and passions, for learning more about them, and for connecting with others who share those interests.

TAKE A MEDIA BREAK: Lola found that she could feel creative and calm when she put her phone on Do

Not Disturb every once in a while. An hour without your phone isn't so bad, and in fact it's healthy: Studies have found that a break from screen time before bed leads to a deeper sleep and then better focus the next day.

Chapter Eight
OPPOSITES ATTRACT

March 5, 1975. It was a cold and drizzly evening in Menlo Park, California. Thirty engineers gathered in a garage. They called themselves the Homebrew Computer Club, and this was their first meeting. Their mission: to make computers accessible to regular people. (This was a big task at a time when most computers were slow, SUV-sized machines that only universities and corporations could afford.)

The garage was chilly, but the engineers left the doors open to the damp night air so people could wander inside. In walked an uncertain young man of twenty-four, a calculator designer for Hewlett-Packard. He had shoulder-length hair, glasses, and a brown beard. Though he was glad to be around some kindred spirits, he didn't talk to anyone in that garage—he was way too shy for that. He took a chair and listened quietly as the others marveled over a new build-it-yourself computer called the Altair 8800, which had recently made the cover of *Popular Electronics* magazine. The Altair wasn't a true personal computer; it was hard to use, and appealed only to the type of person who shows up at a garage on a rainy Wednesday night to talk about microchips. But it was an important first step.

The young man—Stephen Wozniak (or Woz, as he's called by his friends)—was thrilled to hear of the Altair. He had been obsessed with electronics since the age of three. When he was eleven he had come across a magazine article about the first computer, the ENIAC, or Electronic Numerical Integrator and Computer, and ever since, his dream had been to build a machine so small and easy to use that you could keep it at home.

That night he went home and sketched his first design for a personal computer, with a keyboard and a screen just like the kind we use today. It was starting to feel as if The Dream—he thought of it with capital letters—might one day come to pass.

Three months later he built a prototype of that machine. And ten months after that, he and Steve Jobs cofounded Apple Computer.

I'm sure you know Apple as the company that created the iPhone, iPad, MacBook, and many more products. The late Steve Jobs was an outspoken figure in Silicon Valley, California, who eventually became the face of the company. In addition to his genius as a programmer, he was known for his razor-sharp business instincts and charismatic presentations. But Apple began through a partnership of Jobs and Woz. Woz was the one who actually invented the first Apple computer—quietly, behind the scenes—in the first place! Together, these utterly different personality types—one introvert, one extrovert—shaped the Apple brand.

When you read Wozniak's account of his work process on that first PC, the most striking thing is that he was always by himself. He did most of the work inside his cubicle at Hewlett-Packard. He'd arrive around 6:30 a.m. and, alone in the early morning, read engineering magazines, study chip manuals, and prepare designs in his head. After work, he'd go home, make a quick meal, then drive back to the office and work late into the night. For him, this period of quiet nights and solitary sunrises was an amazing and energetic time. His efforts paid off on the night of June 29, 1975 at around 10:00 p.m., when Woz finished building a prototype of his machine. He hit a few keys on the keyboard—and letters appeared on the screen in front of him. It was the sort of breakthrough moment that most of us can only dream of. And he was alone when it happened.

At a moment like that, many people would want to celebrate with their friends, but Woz preferred solitude. His invention changed the technological world, and by partnering with an extrovert who wanted to create a company around Woz's brilliant invention, it made its way into the public eye. There would be no Apple without Steve Jobs, as we all know—but there would also be no Apple without Steve Wozniak.

A POWERFUL PARTNERSHIP

My husband is an outspoken extrovert, and we complement each other in wonderful and unexpected ways. It can be incredibly powerful to partner with someone who is your opposite in disposition. That's what Davis did when he placed his eighth-grade election in the hands of his cheerleading cousin, Jessica.

Or consider the story of James and Brian, students who joined together to win the student council co-presidency at their Manhattan private school. This is how it went down:

As a child, James could often be found happily playing alone. He wasn't antisocial. In fact, he had plenty of friends, but he needed that quiet time to himself, playing with his Pokémon cards and toys. In elementary school James was the starting center back on his soccer team, and the defensive coach on the field, though the role didn't exactly suit him; he felt self-conscious about shouting directions at his teammates. His coach encouraged him to speak up more, but as much as he tried, he never quite felt vocal enough.

James had been at the same school since he was three years old. He got great grades, but just as on the soccer field, he'd often see the standard "needs to speak up more" comments on his report cards. At his middle-school graduation, however, something happened that inspired James to find his own way to step forward. As families and friends gathered for the ceremony beneath an enormous tent, the teachers announced which students were being rewarded for their work in different subjects.

James knew that he'd done very well in French that year, so when his name was called as the top student in that subject, he wasn't surprised. A few minutes later, though, he heard his name again. This time, he'd won the top prize in history. *Two* of the awards? "I was shocked," he said. And his classmates were as well. Even though he'd known most of them for a decade, few knew what a good student he was. Kids kept coming up to congratulate him, and they also confessed that they'd had no idea he was that academic.

The recognition boosted his confidence, allowing him to dream a little bigger. James wanted to become more involved in community service, not to mention contribute to positive changes at the high school, and it seemed as if the best way to achieve these goals would be to run for class president. Needless to say, this was a frightening notion. He wasn't even comfortable leading the defense on his elementary school soccer team. Representing an entire grade of smart, driven students? That was a challenge of another order. And there was an additional wrinkle in his plan. His high school only elected co-presidents, not one student at a time. If he wanted to lead, he would have to find a running mate.

That running mate turned out to be Brian. Brian had been going to James's school since kindergarten, but the two had only recently become friends when they attended the same summer camp and hung out by the lake chatting about sports, girls, and life. When September rolled around, they ate lunch together and chatted online after school. Brian had always seen James as one of the popular kids, since his sportiness had linked him with that group. Brian thought of himself as nerdier. He was the kind of kid who would be more likely to read *National Geographic* than kick a ball around.

You might expect that nerdier Brian would be more shy than athletic James, but not at all. Brian thrived on the energy of the public eye. In classes he was quick to throw up his hand, and in groups he actively sought out the leadership role. He and James were different in almost every way. Brian would soon be eight inches taller than James. And he loved to talk. While James won academic awards at graduation, the students had chosen Brian to speak at the ceremony. He craved the spotlight. James, on the other hand, preferred to work quietly in the background. At some point their conversations started regularly turning to the notion of being class presidents. The more they talked, the more they realized that they were the perfect running mates.

The election process was terrifying to James, though. He already had his platform worked out: He was running in the hope that the school would expand its community service efforts. But the idea of asking people to vote for him was stressful. He was worried that petitioning for support seemed conceited or phony, or that people would think he was running just to boost his résumé and get into a good college. As

James persevered, though, it became obvious that his fears were unfounded. When he pitched his platform to one student at a time, or sometimes in small groups, they'd listen. Without even trying to make an impression, James had already gained a reputation as an honest, passionate person. His classmates trusted him, and they figured that when he *did* choose to speak, he probably had something interesting to say. Plus, he clearly wasn't just seeking attention—he didn't even like attention all that much! He was doing it because he was genuinely ready to take on the responsibilities of student council.

James practiced his speech more times than he could remember, knowing that, unlike his extroverted running mate, he wasn't the sort of person who could simply stand up and freestyle. He was frightened when he walked to the stage, but once his speech began, he grew more comfortable. "The audience started responding in a good way, and I thought, 'I got it.'"

The pair was thrilled when they won the election.

At first, though, Brian struggled to understand his quiet partner. The co-presidents began convening a sort of cabinet meeting of students during which kids could share their ideas and debate different initiatives. Before the meeting, James and Brian would meet to discuss an agenda. James was bursting with ideas in these one-on-one sessions, but once everyone gathered around the table, he seemed to change. Brian would gravitate toward the head of the table and drive the conversation, actively steering the debates, but James would rarely say a word. The other kids started wondering what James was really contributing, or whether he was adding anything at all, and Brian himself began to doubt his friend. "I was a little annoyed, and I told him a few times I wish he did more, but then I realized it's not about doing more and saying more. It's about the meaning behind what you're doing and saying."

Over time, Brian started to see that James interacted with other students on a different level. James devoted his efforts to talking to students individually, including kids outside their grade and circle of friends. Often, these students would have unexpected ideas, and James would bring those proposals to Brian in their private meetings. In one instance, Brian had been pushing to organize a day free of classes, focused entirely on community service, but in cabinet meetings, he was getting a mixed response. At the same time, James had been talking to another student about a class retreat. This boy thought it would be a good idea for the hyper-competitive students to have a day when they were just relaxing, not trying to out-score one another on a test or doing anything that felt like work. The idea resonated with James as well, so he approached Brian and suggested that the kids in their grade could use a chance to bond. Brian took it back to the cabinet. This time they approved, and Brian realized that his friend had a different role to play than his own. James was never going to be loud in their meetings, but he was going to listen, both in the group sessions and in the halls of the school.

Brian came to understand his quiet partner on a deeper

level. "Early on I was comfortable always being the first one to talk and jump out there, but then I was expecting him to follow up and do his own thing and be loud and outgoing," Brian recalled. "It took me a little while to understand that that isn't who he is. Not only is he not comfortable, but that's not what he's good at. That's not his style of leadership."

The more they worked together, the more apparent it was that James and Brian didn't succeed in *spite* of their differences; they succeeded *because* they were opposites. "If he were more like me, we would be much less successful," Brian said. "I wouldn't want him to change. It's beneficial to me, in terms of our friendship and working together, that he's more reserved and more quiet."

There is no right or wrong personality. I celebrate quiet kids and adults because they're often overlooked, but I can't stress enough that introverts and extroverts both have their strengths. And we shouldn't pair up simply because we become more influential or productive. We can also form fantastic friendships. I always had extroverted friends growing up, and there's a great deal to be gained, in terms of maturity, personal growth, and pushing yourself out of your comfort zone, when you're close to different kinds of people. Extroverted Brian has seen that in his relationship with James. "It's nice to have someone like him as a friend. If I want to just have a relaxed and laid-back time, I can do that. We can just hang out for hours playing Ping-Pong and talking."

YIN AND YANG

Through the yin and yang of pairings like James and Brian, you can see how introverts and extroverts can form incredibly powerful partnerships and friendships. Like-minded friends are so special and comforting, but it can be just as interesting, sometimes more so, to hang out with people who are totally different from you. There is so much to learn from them!

Grace has found this to be true, as well. "My two best friends were screaming extroverts," she said. "They liked to go around to different lunch tables and sit with different groups." At first, Grace lacked the confidence to do this on her own. She was worried about what kids would think of her, especially since she was quiet. But her friends made her more comfortable with branching out socially. "They've helped me meet a lot more people. They are always up and going. They're always like, 'Let's go to the pool! Let's go to the library! Let's go to the mall! Let's go everywhere!'"

And yet this friendship was hardly one-sided. Those girls sought out Grace and befriended her because she was refreshingly different from them. The louder girls have also begun to change, now that they've seen some of the advantages of the quiet life. Their parents have gushed to Grace's mother about how she keeps them grounded. Without her, they've joked, the girls might just go spinning off into the universe with all their excess social energy. One night in seventh grade, for example, a big crew of the girls was going out, and Grace declared that she planned to stay home. She realized that she needed a mellow night. Sure enough, to her mother's shock, one of those screaming extroverts, the kind of girl who would never miss an outing, decided to follow Grace's lead. She told the others that she wasn't going to join them, saying, "I want to hang with Grace."

According to the pediatrician Marianne Kuzujanakis, young people are drawn to their opposites because they have qualities they admire but lack in themselves. She mentioned an introverted nine-year-old boy she knew well who was great friends with an extroverted girl. He liked her for her outgoing, energetic personality, and admired her ability to go right up to people and talk to them. Yet the girl benefitted from their friendship just as much. "She'd observe him and see that it was okay to be quiet. She liked him for his calmness." The pair took tai chi classes together, and even in that environment, their differing strengths were clear. "She appreciated how he was good at the meditation aspect, how that came naturally to him, and he was amazed at how she interacted so easily with everyone in the group."

A few years ago, a psychologist named Avril Thorne set up an experiment to explore the social interactions between introverts and extroverts. Thorne was looking in particular at how the two groups connected on the phone. The experiment brought together fifty-two young women—half were introverted, half extroverted—and paired them in conversations. Many people assume introverts are quiet all the time, but the study revealed that they talk just as much as their personality opposites. (Any one of my high school friends could tell you this, as we talked for hours on the phone—that's what kids did back then—each night.) In the experiment, when introverts talked to other introverts, they tended to focus on one or a few deep or profound subjects. When extroverts were matched up with other extroverts, on the other hand, they tended to gloss over a whole range of topics, without digging too deeply into one particular subject. The really interesting results popped up when introverts and extroverts were paired together. Both groups reported that these conversations were the most enjoyable. People preferred talking to their opposites. The introverts found that talking to someone chattier made the conversation a little more lighthearted and fun. The extroverted women in the group said they found the conversations more serious and deep. In effect, the women ended up meeting halfway, and finding the right mix of lighthearted chatter and deep conversation.

PAIRING WITH EXTROVERTS

Besides learning from one another, introverts and extroverts often find that they balance each other out. As you get to know people who are different and more extroverted than you, consider these tips:

RECOGNIZE YOUR WORTH: Don't be afraid to befriend people who are more outgoing than you. They will value your thoughtfulness and calm, and will gain as much from you as you will from them.

OBSERVE AND LEARN: I'm not suggesting that you approach your friendship with an extrovert as some kind of tutorial, but do try to learn from them, and try to find ways to expand your comfort zone. And let them learn from you too!

KNOW YOUR LIMITS: Stretch yourself by meeting new people, heading out to parties, and wandering into other extrovert-friendly territory, but be aware of your internal needs as well. Take a break when you want to; stay in when all the others are heading out if that's what you need.

CHANNEL SOMEONE WHO HAS THE SKILLS YOU NEED: Be inspired by the yin to your yang. Is there someone you follow on Twitter who always has the wittiest comebacks? Or a relative who always seems to have energy to spare? Think about what they'd do or what kind of advice they'd give you.

PART THREE
HOBBIES

Chapter Nine
QUIET CREATIVITY

Many introverts say they struggle to express themselves around others. So in this chapter, we'll talk about the many ways to communicate feelings and ideas other than in conversation.

You've probably noticed already that your personal interests keep growing through the years—and that creativity comes in many forms. It can express itself through drawing or composing music, through writing code or brainstorming ideas for a new app or entrepreneurial idea. Or through many other media besides. Creativity is limitless.

Remember Karinah, from chapter 1—the reserved fifteen-year-old from Brooklyn? She also happens to be an extremely creative person. When she finds something that deeply interests her, she pursues it with all her heart. Recently, she noticed someone at her church playing a guitar, and her admiration for that instrument led her to start teaching herself the ukulele, a smaller string instrument. Now, when Karinah's not practicing TV theme songs on her ukulele, she's writing new melodies to go with her original song lyrics.

But first and foremost, Karinah's passion is writing. She is practically addicted to coming up with ideas for novels and short stories. Sci-fi and fantasy are her favorite genres to read and to write. With her ability to focus for hours at a time, she labors over her laptop, outlining new stories and illustrating characters in her secret notebook. When she feels that a story is polished enough, she shares it on a young writers' site. "It's for other people to comment on what I put up. I don't want to be forceful or ask for attention. I want you to read it and see if you like it, and maybe add some constructive criticism."

Karinah's school doesn't have the funding for art or creative writing classes, so one of the language teachers decided to do something that would support its many creative students. She started a monthly event in her classroom called Coffee Shop. Coffee Shop is an open-mike event, where students are invited to bring a poem, song, rap, or other type of performance that they're working on, and share it with their peers. Since it's participant-run, the only people who show up are the ones who *want* to be there. It makes for a supportive, enthusiastic environment—and Karinah was amazed to find herself sharing her work in public—and to realize how much people *loved* her writing! At first, when she read her work aloud, she kept her eyes glued on her paper. But occasionally she'd glance up and notice her friends' eyes bugging out in suspense at a creepy part, or laughing at the sly, sarcastic dialogue she wrote for her characters. They were reacting even better than she'd expected. They got it!

Her teacher recognized Karinah's skills and encouraged her to apply to Girls Write Now, a New York City program in which teenage girls work on their creative writing one-on-one with mentors who are women writers. Once a month, all the participants meet up for workshops on topics such as poetry writing and journalism. Karinah was accepted into the program, and she found that she was interested in sharing her work and in hearing other girls' writing at the workshops. At first, sharing with strangers was nerve-racking, but it also felt like a precious opportunity to grow as a writer. Getting feedback in person from other writers her age, as well as from grown-ups, was a revelation. Karinah took comfort in hearing the words and thoughts of creative peers of all ages.

Sharing your written or artistic work, like performing on a stage, can take a lot of courage. We introverts might not seem to want to broadcast our thoughts or talents to the world, but when we do, the results can be spectacular.

Take this example of a quiet young woman named Jo who boarded a train for Scotland one day. As she gazed out the window at fields full of cows, she suddenly imagined a *boy* riding on a train, heading to a school for aspiring wizards. This school was filled with all kinds of imaginary characters—friends, enemies, sorcerers, and mythical creatures. It took Jo several years and countless rewrites and struggles, but she kept working, and she finally had a typed, complete manuscript. Two years after that, her novel was finally published. It was called *Harry Potter and the Sorcerer's Stone*, and the book's introverted author, J. K. Rowling, would go on to write six more novels about the boy on the train.

DEAR DIARY

"Writing is something you do alone," says bestselling author John Green. "It's a profession for introverts who want to tell you a story but don't want to make eye contact while doing it."

When I was younger, my chosen medium was an old-fashioned diary, complete with lock and key. While I did write stories from time to time, the diary was my place for truth and confession. It existed apart from the world—I never shared it with friends or family. It helped me organize and make sense of the anxieties of my childhood and teen years. If anyone had read my diary, it would have been an earth-shattering event. But this habit of expressing myself on the page trained me to be an honest writer.

A diary doesn't have to come in the form of a bound and sealed notebook. Maggie keeps a note on her phone that she adds to daily. "I like to write down my dreams so I remember them. I write about ideas I have or things that made me excited but I'm afraid to jinx if I share them with anyone out loud."

As a high schooler, Jared from California free-wrote on his computer. "That was my resource," he said. "It was my way to survive when my head was exploding. A lot of it was anxieties, very personal thoughts about people or situations or struggles I was going through. It was a way to release the tension." He barely reread what he wrote. He'd hammer out his thoughts on the keyboard, then get ready to sleep. "I would write, brush my teeth, and go to bed," he said. "My mind might still be buzzing but it wasn't buzzing as much. It would be a weight lifted off my shoulders."

THE RELUCTANT BLOGGER

Still, writing doesn't appeal to everyone. A shy New Jersey teen named Matthew was annoyed when his teacher instructed the class to start their own blogs. Matthew was more into science and math than English, and he thought the blog entries were going to be just another writing assignment, like a book report. It turned out that students could write about whatever they wanted. Once Matthew set the background to an image of the classic video game Legend of Zelda, he felt more at home. "It was more of a creative outlet than I'd expected," he said. "I could really express myself."

Normally, Matthew remained quiet in classroom discussions. He followed along, but he could never formulate his responses in time, or with enough confidence, to contribute. As a result, he didn't often share his thoughts, ideas, and interests. The blog gave him an outlet—and it gave him time. He could write at his own speed. One of his entries was about his passion for K-pop, Korean pop music. He posted a video of one of his favorite songs, and a few people commented. A girl in his class approached him to say that she shared his taste, and this sparked a messaging exchange. "We didn't know each other that much, but we've talked a lot more than we normally would have," he recalled later. "We've actually become pretty good friends."

At the end of the school year, Matthew wrote about how much he enjoyed expressing himself online, then joked that maybe blogging was part of a media conspiracy to convert introverts into extroverts. But of course, he hasn't converted. His personality hasn't changed. Matt was *always* funny and lively; he has just discovered a new, more comfortable way to share that side of himself.

ART

Jaden is a twelve-year-old with a wild imagination who sometimes struggles to connect the world *inside* his head to the one *outside*. So he looked for a way to enjoy the sanctuary of his mind while sharing his imagination with others.

He found that balance in drawing, especially fantastical images like dragons. He'll think about something while in school—sometimes during math class, he admits—or while on his skateboard, and then when he gets home, he'll put it down on paper. "Recently I drew this landscape, and there's a unicorn with a griffin above it and they're in this weird waterfall place," Jaden says with a laugh. "My friends think it's amazing. A lot of them draw too, and we've started showing our work to each other. For me it feels really good to share, because everyone's seeing what's inside my head."

For Julian, his creativity comes through in photography. "Looking at Instagram used to make me feel kind of excluded from cool stuff other kids were doing. Then I realized that I didn't *have* to flip through other people's photos and stare at a screen. Instead, I could actually learn to take great pictures myself." That's how he and his best friend, Andre, decided to get into capturing artistic and beautiful photos. "We go out on photo shoots together just with our phones. We'll go to the park, or the beach, or by the canal in Red Hook in Brooklyn. We can find pictures anywhere. There's interesting stuff all over. They're not just recording moments and people, they're about framing something beautiful, or contrasting light. It's about appreciating random things and making it meaningful." By making something artistic out of the little things he observes, Julian has created photos he's proud of. He gets more out of them than just likes on Instagram—he gets a sense of creative pride.

Introverts contribute enormously to the creative arts. Pixar, the innovative animation studio behind such films as *Toy Story; Monsters, Inc.;* and *Inside Out,* has an introvert, Ed Catmull, at its helm. And the Pixar director Pete Docter says that, as a kid, drawing helped him deal with his "fear of connecting with other people. It was a means of escape, creating my own little universe by myself." Docter has also noted that working with his Pixar crew is draining as well as thrilling. When he was working on the film *Monsters, Inc.,* he says, "By the end of the day, I just wanted to be by myself. I wanted to go retreat into my basement, or under my desk or something." In fact, his idea for the hit film *Up* was inspired by a daydream I think a lot of introverts have: of floating away from our surroundings to somewhere safe and alone.

THE POWER OF INDEPENDENCE

Introverts have a remarkable ability to be independent. We find strength in solitude, and are capable of using our precious alone time to focus and concentrate.

A sports commentator once referred to this as "the lonely work" that needs to be completed in order to master a skill. Psychologists call it by another name: "deliberate practice." In simple terms, it means practicing something over and over again, always focusing on the skill that's just out of reach, until you get it exactly right.

Whatever title you use, it turns out that focused, deliberate, often solitary work is crucial to mastery of pretty much any pursuit you can name, including team sports.

We introverts are especially suited to solitary practice, in music, sports, and other pursuits. The basketball star Kobe Bryant, for example, used to shoot one thousand jump shots every day. The young pianist Conrad Tao, who played in front of a packed house at New York's famous Carnegie Hall when he was only seventeen years old, spent most of his teen years alone in his family apartment, honing his skills at the keys while his parents were at work. The homeschooled musician would spend four hours at the piano and two on the violin before even starting his normal academic studies.

And then there's Steve Wozniak, the Apple inventor you met in the last chapter. Woz says that he practiced engineering ever since he was a little kid. In his memoir *iWoz*, he describes his passion for electronics. He built his expertise step by painstaking step, entering countless science fairs. "I acquired a central ability that was to help me through my entire career: patience. . . . I learned to not worry so much about the outcome, but to concentrate on the step I was on and to try to do it as perfectly as I could."

Woz often worked alone. A famously friendly guy, he had plenty of friends during elementary school. But like many technically inclined kids, he took a painful tumble down the social ladder when he got to middle school. As a boy he'd been admired for his science prowess, but now nobody seemed to care. He hated small talk, and his interests were out of step with those of his peers. But the awkwardness of his middle-school years didn't deter him from pursuing his dream; it probably nurtured it. He would never have learned so much about computers, Woz says now, if he hadn't been too shy to leave the house.

No one would choose this sort of painful adolescence, but the fact is that the solitude of Woz's teens, and his single-minded focus on what would turn out to be a lifelong passion, is typical for highly creative people. According to the psychologist Mihaly Csikszentmihalyi, who between 1990 and 1995 studied the lives of ninety-one exceptionally creative people in the arts, sciences, business, and government, many of his subjects were on the social margins during adolescence, partly because "intense curiosity or focused interest seems odd to their peers." Teens who are too gregarious to spend time alone often fail to cultivate their talents "because practicing music or studying math requires a solitude they dread."

THE INTROVERTED MAESTRO

Meet Maria, a California middle-schooler whose story is all about doing "the lonely work." Maria found school exhausting. She was so worn out by the end of each morning that she'd climb a tree at lunch and eat by herself. Some of her closest friends were her total opposites. They were loud and boisterous and happiest in big groups. They thought her hiding-in-a-tree time was weird, but Maria didn't care. For her, it was a necessary part of the school day. Up in the branches, she could recharge her batteries for the afternoon's activities.

Maria's comfort with solitude allowed her to develop some productive hobbies. She wrote a ten-thousand-word story when she was only ten years old, and she practiced the fiddle diligently. In particular, Maria loved bluegrass and Celtic fiddling, two traditions that involve circles or even crowds of musicians jamming together. She decided that she wanted to play with other musicians in one of these groups, and her mother, though surprised, supported her quest. Since Maria was too young for the bars where these musicians typically gather, they searched for other venues. In one of their first adventures, they drove to a park where a group of fiddlers played on Sunday afternoons.

"If your daughter is mute, you should tell us," one of the members said after the music session. "We're more than happy to be accommodating, but it's very difficult to work with someone who has a disability and not know it."

"She's not mute," Maria's mother corrected. "She's shy." They searched elsewhere.

They tracked down a fiddling session in an artsy café not far from their home. One weekend afternoon, they arrived while the group was already playing. Maria's mother left her daughter in charge. She took a seat at a table nearby, close enough to listen and chime in if necessary.

The members of the group were all different ages and ethnicities, yet Maria was the youngest by at least forty years. She pulled up a chair and got ready to play. When the banjo player changed keys, everyone else had to switch as well, and the musicians would take turns

picking a song in that key. Before long, the organizer of the group, an older woman, turned to Maria. "Well, it's your turn," she said. "What do you know in B?"

"It's okay," Maria said. "You can pass me."

The woman shook her head. "We don't take passes. Can you think of anything in B?"

"No," Maria replied.

Maria's mother knew that when her daughter gave that monosyllabic reply, she meant it. There was no point in trying to push her.

But this woman did not know Maria, and she wasn't going to let that simple no stop her. "Okay," she said, "I'm going to start to play some songs in B, and when I get to a song you know, tell me to stop. And then you're going to lead that song."

The woman started playing. Maria listened hard. A few songs in, she started nodding. "I know that one," she said.

"Great," the woman said. "Now lead it."

As Maria led the musicians, her mother watched, radiant

with pride. When Maria got home from the jam session, she rushed to her room to make a list of all the songs she knew, organized by key. She brought it to the next fiddle session. Eventually the woman in charge knew to ask, "What's on the list, Maria?"

Maria didn't like being singled out in a group, but playing music made her feel creative and excited, and she could express herself through the melodies. So she gathered her strength and overcame her shyness. Her introverted nature might appear to have been a drawback in that situation, but in fact it was the reason she was able to fit in so easily. Her dedication to the instrument, and the joy she experienced from practicing every day on her own, allowed her to become a better player with a more attuned ear. She didn't blend into that group of adult musicians in spite of her quiet nature. She blended in *because* she was introverted. And her fan base kept growing. When news of Maria's skills as a fiddler spread around the school, students started approaching the school's music teacher. They asked him to talk Maria into starting a band with them.

EXPRESSING YOURSELF THE QUIET WAY

One of introverts' great superpowers is our ability to dive deeply into a project and focus for long stretches. Combine this with our creative drive, and the results can be powerful, leading us down unexpected and quite wonderful paths. You may choose to keep the results of these excursions under lock and key, or you may want to share them with the world. But either way, learning to express yourself with honesty, confidence, and heart will be so rewarding.

Here are a few pointers, gathered in one place, to get you started:

FIND YOUR MEDIUM: Maybe you'll discover an app for creating beats, or a recipe that inspires you to bake something totally new. Maybe all you need is a sharpened pencil for writing or drawing. Try to identify the means of self-expression that feels natural and exciting to you.

PRODUCE: Once you've identified this calling, pursue it with energy and passion. Throw yourself into it. Practice, practice, practice.

SEEK INSPIRATION IN ROLE MODELS AND ALLIES: Finding role models who are also introverted can show you that your goals are achievable. There are people just like you who have been widely recognized for their creativity, charisma, and intelligence. (Many are profiled on the Quiet Revolution website, Quietrev.com.)

CLAIM PRIVACY: Some diaries are never meant to be read, and some projects are for you and you alone. Create a safe space to write or create without worrying about what anyone else thinks. Enjoy having projects all to yourself . . .

BUT DON'T FORGET TO SHARE: Let others see and hear what's going on inside your head. Often, people hesitate to share because they're afraid of criticism. But try showing your work to a friend or two. Feedback can be helpful, and you might be surprised by how supportive and appreciative people can be.

Chapter Ten
THE QUIET ATHLETE

A college student named Maggie used to think of sports as a pursuit for popular jocks. It was off-limits to a bookish person like her, as far as she could tell. But that was before she discovered yoga in ninth grade. The sun salutations and stretches she practiced in her room, after being inspired by a podcast she'd heard, gave her a boost of cheer in the morning before getting on the bus.

Introverts like us are sometimes so deep in our heads that escaping into our bodies can be a welcome and healthy change of pace. Exercising and sweating are great ways to release social anxiety and frustration and to promote mental well-being. That's because exercising releases endorphins. Endorphins are chemicals that our brains produce in response to certain kinds of stimulation. They can block feelings of pain, and also enhance feelings of joy. And athletics aren't all about rowdy cheers or team spirit—solo sports such as running, swimming, and fencing are a great way for introverts to release energy and taste a piece of that euphoria.

An introverted girl we spoke with named Brittany told us about how she turned to dance. She had always loved dancing, but the traditional, crowded school affair felt too awkward for her. When she was fourteen, though, her brother introduced her to swing, the 1940s style of dancing with a partner that had become popular again. She was so taken with swing that she convinced an older friend of hers to drive her to a swing dancing session every Friday night at a dance hall. The other dancers were as young as twelve and as old as ninety, but shy Brittany would partner with all of them. "It was a friendly environment, and dancing gave you something in common. You didn't have to focus on what you were saying. You didn't have to say *anything* if you didn't want to. You could just dance and laugh and be silly," she recalled. Afterward, Brittany and her friend would go out to eat with some of the other dancers. Being sweaty and carefree together on the dance floor was enough of an icebreaker that Brittany didn't even feel nervous sitting around a table with a group of people. She found herself connecting in new ways, not just through clever conversation or by looking cool.

THE POWER OF VISUALIZATION

Ever since Jeff was a little kid, he loved to practice playing sports alone. He'd dribble a soccer ball or try to catch pop flies in baseball all by himself. Sure, the endorphin rush was amazing, but above all, Jeff enjoyed that time to himself. Growing up in a small town outside Albany, New York, he loved most sports, and excelled at soccer, but it wasn't until he started playing lacrosse that something inside him clicked. Lacrosse was meant for him.

At thirteen, though, he had some catching up to do. Some of his peers had already mastered the use of the lacrosse stick to catch and throw with both their left and right hands. He needed to catch up with them—maybe even surpass them.

Jeff started practicing every day. He'd run over to his old elementary school, set himself in front of a bare concrete wall, and throw the ball to himself hundreds—maybe even thousands—of times a day. His skills and his confidence blossomed. He had a gut feeling that he was working harder than anyone he was playing against, and that gave him an edge. By his junior year of high school, Jeff set a school record for points in a season. During his senior year, he was named an All-American, one of the highest honors for a high school player.

The following year, Jeff enrolled at West Point, a four-year military academy known for its rigorous training. There, his enthusiasm for lacrosse only grew. The two- to three-hour practices were a welcome break from the intense life of a cadet, and Jeff would often spend extra time training on his own after official practices. During his junior year, he worked with a West Point psychologist who helped athletes improve their performances. He was surprised to realize how fascinating psychology could be. There was so much to learn about the power of positive thinking, the importance of setting goals, and how to stay calm and play well under pressure.

What truly caught Jeff's attention was a technique called visualization. This required quiet focus and imagination: In his head, Jeff would play a mental video of what he *hoped* would happen on the field. When he was in the psychologist's office, he would watch highlight reels of his own games and imagine himself making his best plays again.

Prior to big games, Jeff and his assistant coach would watch videos of the team's opponents to better understand how they played. Jeff looked for holes in their defensive schemes, or bad tendencies on the part of the players, then imagined himself exploiting them, rushing past them for a goal or an easy assist to a teammate. Then, right before the games, while some of his teammates were yelling or shouting to get themselves ready, Jeff would quietly put on his headphones, sit by himself, and start visualizing. He'd recall those old highlight reels, and in his mind he'd run through the opponents' defense, making play after play. Those last two years of Jeff's college career, when he'd mastered visualization, were his best ones as an athlete. He was twice named to the All-American team and he broke the West Point record for assists in a season.

SOLITUDE ON THE ICE—AND IN THE WATER

There are introverts in every sport, but we often gravitate to those that allow us to play or practice on our own, like swimming, cross-country running, and golf. As a kid, I was no exception. At age ten, I started figure skating competitively. The sport held a special appeal for me. There was something magical about watching a skater glide, spin, and jump across the ice. I wanted to be part of that beautiful world, and although I began skating too late to have Olympic dreams, the simple act of trying to improve excited me. The hours I spent on the ice, practicing in solitude, were pure bliss. My mind would drift to the events of the day, and the worries and stresses of my life would start to seem less important. "In a way, the sport becomes a form of meditation," says the psychologist Elizabeth Mika. "It occupies your body so that your mind has time for introspection."

Jenny, a quiet teenager from Seattle, similarly enjoys the meditative appeal of swimming. She tried a variety of sports as she was growing up. In middle school, she and her friend both played on a soccer team stacked with loud, cheering girls. The team would go bananas when they scored a goal, but Jenny couldn't bring herself to imitate their rambunctiousness. "One girl would always get mad at me. She'd be like, 'Why aren't you participating? Why don't you care?'"

Soon Jenny gave up soccer in favor of swimming. "It was just really calming to be in this space in your own head," she said. "When I would start out, for the first few laps my mind would be crazy, going through random topics. And then once I got to a certain point it would just kind of blank out. If I had a fight with my friend and I was feeling really sad, I would either swim it out and forget about it for a minute, and use the exercise to clear my mind, or I would just kind of think while I swam."

The sports psychologist Alan Goldberg, who has worked with both amateur athletes and Olympians, says that it's common to find introverts in the pool. "Swimming is the kind of sport that attracts people who can tolerate the quiet," he said. "By nature the sport demands that you have the ability to tolerate long hours of just being with yourself and not really interacting."

INTROSPECTIVE ON THE MOUND

Despite the draw of solitary sports, introverted athletes can excel on any playing field or court. Two of the best point guards in the National Basketball Association, Derrick Rose and Rajon Rondo, have been described as highly introverted. In fact, one of Rose's greatest skills, according to his coach, is that he's an excellent listener.

Similarly, the soccer stars Lionel Messi and Cristiano Ronaldo are both known for working harder than everyone else, using the principles of deliberate practice to make their games better and better.

And the entire Washington Nationals baseball team has been described (in a 2012 newspaper article) as leaning toward the introverted side of the personality spectrum. These athletes were generally sociable, but also analytical, focused, and introspective. As a team, they didn't celebrate the loud guys who always needed to have the last word. Even their manager at the time, Davey Johnson, observed that he preferred meeting with players one-on-one to the standard team-wide clubhouse sessions.

Nina, a high school softball player from Ohio, knows all about the solitary work it takes to be great. She played a variety of sports when she was younger, including soccer and basketball, but softball had always been her hands-down favorite. Nina is a pitcher, and a ferocious one at that. Once, she hurled the ball so hard that she broke her father's finger when they were playing catch in the backyard.

Nina practiced her sport every day. She ran in the hills near her home and stayed late after team practices, working on her flaws. She'd even hone her skills while sitting at home watching TV: She would typically have a softball in her hand, trying out different grips and spins so that she could master new pitches. Either that or she'd pick up a dumbbell and work on strengthening her wrists. As a junior, Nina threw a no-hitter, which means she pitched an entire game without a single player on the opposing squad earning a hit. The next year, as a senior, she improved further in almost every category.

BEATING BRONZE

Of course, there's also a downside to being an introverted athlete, observes sports psychologist Alan Goldberg. Introverts often have a tendency to overthink what they're doing, Goldberg says, and to be harder on themselves when they make a mistake or miss a goal.

I very much relate to this point. Back when I was a figure skater, I struggled mightily with competitions. I could spend hours on the rink during practice sessions, skating perfectly. But on the big day, I was a wreck. I couldn't sleep the night before, and when it was my turn to skate I'd fall during moves that I had sailed through in practice. It took me many years to grow comfortable as a performer and competitor. (Hopefully, you won't have to wait so long! If I had to do it again, I would know myself better, and give myself more practice with performance itself: During the lead-up to a big competition, I would take as many dress rehearsals as I needed to become accustomed to the feel of skating under a spotlight.)

Hans Rombaut, a black belt in tae kwon do, had a similar problem. He first became passionate about the martial arts when he was ten years old. He wasn't bullied, so his interest had nothing to do with self-defense. No, he wanted to learn martial arts because he was obsessed with Bruce Lee and the Teenage Mutant Ninja Turtles. Even though soccer and cycling were the most popular sports in his native Belgium, he was desperate to try martial arts, and his parents reluctantly allowed it. By the time he was fourteen years old, he was practicing several hours a day.

Hans enjoyed the long periods of hard work and chose the more solitary form of tae kwon do. He ended up specializing in the choreography portion, which means he didn't actually fight anyone in his matches. Instead, he would perform a series of moves alongside another competitor. A panel of judges would score the two demonstrations based on which competitor had the best technique, the sharpest kicks, and so on. In tournaments, the individual with the highest score would move to the next round.

The discipline was perfect for introverted Rombaut, since it required solitary training and performance. He steadily improved, and within a few years had earned a spot on Belgium's national team. Yet his success soon tailed off. "Once I was on the national team I would always end up with a bronze," he said. "People were calling me Mr. Bronze!" He had no difficulty winning the early rounds of the competitions, but the pressure set in when he neared the finals. The thought of performing in front of hundreds of spectators was too much for him to bear: He would overthink his match, freeze up, and lose in the semifinal round.

After years of disappointing results, Hans began working with a coach who focused on this mental roadblock. She convinced Hans to disregard the crowds, and the judges too. "I'd tell myself, 'There is no one here. Just me and my coach. And this is just a demonstration for her to see where I'm at,'" he said. "Once I lowered the pressure mentally, that's when I started to get my best results." Within a year, Hans had won the European championships.

When the judges announced his victory, his whole team rushed the competition mat and cheered. At that moment, the spotlight didn't bother Hans at all. "It was crowded. Everyone was watching. But I didn't mind. It was just euphoria."

If you can overcome the stress of competition and avoid the trap of overthinking, like Hans, then being introverted can be an enormous advantage for you as an athlete. You possess three critical superpowers: tolerance for solitary practice, a quest for perfection, and intense focus.

But sports don't have to be all about competition. Take Julian, whose diverse interests range from piano to photography to—most recently—martial arts. He's training his body by practicing parkour, which is the martial art of running away. "It's learning how to utilize your body best in the environment you're in. So if there are walls, it's about getting over the walls, learning how to land, jumping off of things, and rolling and falling. I love it because it's something I can do on my own. It's about testing your *own* strength, not necessarily competing with others. I read about it and watch videos, and just try to copy."

If you love an activity for the sheer joy of movement—or of pursuing excellence—don't fall into the trap of thinking that the only way to express this dedication is through competition. That's one way to do it. But it's not the only one.

THE INTROVERTED ATHLETE'S GAME PLAN

Adolescence is a time when your body is changing. Show it some love. Test out what works for you. You might find that raising your heart rate and getting a little sweaty relaxes you and gets you out of your head. Think about exercise in this way: The important thing isn't body weight or some unfair standard of beauty—it's mental clarity and that happy feeling of released endorphins. You might not be one of the loudest athletes on the court, but you *could* be the one who earns the loudest cheers.

PRACTICE ALONE: Embrace solitude as a time to both enhance your skills and restore your mental energy.

STUDY YOUR GAME: Channel your ability to focus, and apply that to your sport. Build a deeper understanding of your game or event. Use the principles of deliberate practice (that likely come naturally to you) to improve and excel.

VISUALIZE SUCCESS: Put your busy, imaginative brain to work by picturing your victory and bolstering your confidence.

SHRINK YOUR WORLD: Don't let the crowd sap your energy and strength, as it did for Hans. *Forget* the crowd. Shrink your world down to the mat, the field, or the pool. Block out the external distractions and focus entirely on your performance.

EXERCISE SOLO: Yoga, running, walking, climbing, sit-ups. These are all exercises you can do for free, on your own, in your bedroom or outside.

Chapter Eleven
QUIETLY ADVENTUROUS

Growing up in Australia, Jessica Watson and her siblings weren't homeschooled. They were boat-schooled. When Jessica was in the fifth grade, her parents bought a fifty-two-foot boat, packed the kids on board, and set off on what became a five-year-long adventure around the coast of Australia. Jessica was a quiet girl, but underneath her shy exterior, an adventurous spirit was blossoming. When she returned home at the age of eleven, she learned about the sailor Jesse Martin, who sailed around the world by himself in 1999 when he was only eighteen years old. Martin's story shook Jessica to her core. Even at her young age, she knew that this kind of journey was for her. She too wanted to sail around the world. And she wanted to do it alone.

At first, Jessica kept her dream to herself. Who would take it seriously? But she secretly started researching what's known as solo sailing, learning everything she could about the difficult art of piloting a sailboat without help. She pictured what it would be like to be caught in a perilous storm on the open sea. What would such danger feel like? Would she be up for the challenge? Could she manage being alone for an entire lap around the earth? She turned herself into an expert on weather, navigation, and equipment. The more she researched and daydreamed, the more confident she felt that she'd be able to handle whatever Mother Nature threw her way.

Jessica was determined to sail the world, and believe it or not . . . she actually convinced her parents to let her. This voyage required *serious* planning. She lined up sponsors and recruited a team of experts to chart and follow her journey. She tricked out her boat, called the *Ella's Pink Lady*, with the right equipment to keep her safe and prepared for wild and unpredictable weather. Then, on October 18, 2009, she set out on her own. She was sixteen years old and planning to spend the next *nine months* solo. Thanks to some remarkable communications gear, she would have Wi-Fi for talking to friends, family members, and her support team; she could even check Facebook now and then.

Yet she was still going to be completely, utterly alone out there on the open sea.

Jessica set off on her journey. Once she lost sight of the shore, she found that the solitude didn't bother her. Sure, she talked to her weather vane, the instrument that measures the direction of the breeze (and she even named it Parker). And she had conversations with a seabird that decided to hang out on the boat for a little while, spoke on occasion with the stuffed animals she'd brought along, and gave the boat itself pep talks, addressing the ship as if it were a real person needing encouragement in the face of a coming storm. There were some emotional downtimes, but amazingly, while she did use the phone often to check in with friends and family, there were still times when she turned down a chance to talk, preferring the silence. And she found that her older brother could still annoy her from thousands of miles away. At one point, while she was alone in the middle of the Pacific Ocean, she wrote on her blog, "Thanks to Dad and Bruce over the last few days for being so patient with me over the phone and for understanding that sometimes a girl just doesn't feel like chatting!"

The journey amazed her; she had experiences that sound like a dream. Pods of dolphins swam around her bow. Miniature squid somehow fell onto the deck at night. She saw a nocturnal rainbow, known as a moonbow, as the moonlight shone through a storm.

There was also a run-in with a tanker ship and damage to the boat. There were massive waves that washed over the boat, turning it on its side and tossing her around in the cabin like a waterlogged doll. One night she accidentally boiled her pasta dinner in diesel fuel. So many people on land had said that she shouldn't take this voyage, that she wouldn't be able to handle it. Even in moments of vulnerability and fear, though, Jessica deeply knew that she could in fact handle it.

And so she endured, with great energy and dedication. After sailing 24,285 miles over 210 days, she pulled into Sydney, Australia, to a welcome brigade that included helicopters, boats, television crews, crowds, and, of course, her family. Jessica had become the youngest person to ever sail solo around the world.

THE LARGEST DOSE OF LEMON JUICE

There's a tendency to think of adventurers as rough and tumble, bold, and brash. Often, though, the greatest challenges on grand journeys demand an unexpected set of skills. To complete Jessica's incredible adventure, she needed the ability to focus intently, a high tolerance for solitude, and plenty of emotional strength. As an introvert, Jessica was ideally suited to the task.

In general, though, *extroverts* are more likely to be drawn to risky situations. It's not that introverts don't take risks, because they do. But they tend to be more careful and measured about the risks they take.

Some scientists believe that the reason people enjoy taking risks may relate to a phenomenon called reward-sensitivity. Typically, we look to challenges as a way to gain some kind of reward, whether it's the satisfaction of climbing a mountain or the prize that comes with a winning raffle ticket. There's evidence that extroverts are more susceptible to the rush of pride, excitement, and all-around positive feelings that come with achieving a goal, winning a competition, or overcoming impossible odds. Sure, we all enjoy that thrill. But scientists have found that extroverts experience a slightly more intense kick. The human brain has a kind of built-in reward system, a network of pathways that send signals back and forth, through a chemical called dopamine, to boost our excitement when something good happens. Scientists say that dopamine pathways appear to be more active in the brains of extroverts.

In one study, researchers looked at introverts and extroverts who won gambling contests, and the extroverted winners had more activity in the reward areas of their brains than the introverted victors. I'm sure the introverts loved winning too. But the evidence suggests that their brains' reward networks were just a little less activated, so they felt a bit more mellow about the experience.

Other studies have found that extroverts drive more rashly and get into more car accidents than introverts do!

When it comes to dangerous adventures like sailing the world or climbing a mountain, introverts' mellowness can be enormously useful. Consider the research of Gunnar Breivik, a sociologist in Norway who has been studying the personalities of extreme sports athletes for decades. At one point Breivik studied mountain climbers as they scaled rock faces, snowy peaks, and steep indoor rock walls. In several studies, he found that climbers were often calmer, more introspective types who would quietly visualize what they wanted to pursue. The ones who were drawn to climbing in nature rather than in the gymnasium were especially introverted.

In another project, Breivik examined the personalities of the members of a 1985 Norwegian expedition to Mount Everest. The group was very successful compared to other Everest climbers. Six of the seven Norwegian adventurers completed the trek and reached the summit. Breivik assumed they would tend more toward the extroverted end of the spectrum, given the extreme sensations that came with braving the intense cold, winds, and snow. Remember the lemon juice study that found that introverts react more intensely to stimulation and are more easily overwhelmed by it? Well, Everest represented stimulation at its most intense—the largest dose of lemon juice in the world. Plus, the expedition required incredible cooperation, and he figured that extroverts would be better at working as a team.

As it turned out, though, the adventurers were largely introverted. "They were independent, self-willed, imaginative types," he said. Yet they were also able to work together to help one another reach the top of the world's highest mountain.

Jessica Watson and her amazing solo sail helped to prove Breivik's point that adventurers are often highly focused introverts. Jessica was so competent out at sea in part because her quiet nature allowed her to remain calm and focused on the dangers at hand. Even on such a risky journey, she managed to stay safe by concentrating on accurate directions, maneuvering through the turbulent ocean waves, and taking care of herself on her own terms.

THE SCIENTIST WITH A NOSE FOR OBSERVATION

Other introverted adventurers aren't natural risk takers, but are willing to stretch themselves, and face great danger, in the service of a passion or project. The young Charles Darwin, one of history's most influential introverts, developed the theory of evolution, which speculated that all species have developed over time to suit their environments. It completely changed our understanding of human nature and biology. As a boy, Darwin was fond of long, solitary walks, and he'd fish for hours by himself. Occasionally, his introspective nature got him into trouble. Once, while wandering the countryside in his native England, he became so wrapped up in his own thoughts that he walked right off the edge of a path and fell to the ground some eight feet below!

As a young student of science, Darwin yearned to see the world beyond Great Britain, and in the summer of 1831, he got his chance. The British government had commissioned a ship, the *Beagle*, to explore the waters off the coast of South America. The captain, Robert FitzRoy, wanted a geologist on board to study the landscape. One of Darwin's former professors suggested him, and after some initial hesitation, Charles accepted. The captain was reluctant to bring the young man along, however. He was skeptical of Darwin's introverted nature, and he believed that you could judge a man's character by his appearance—especially by the shape of his facial features. Captain FitzRoy didn't think that anyone with a nose shaped like Darwin's would have the energy and determination needed to complete such a voyage!

He finally agreed, though, and the *Beagle* set sail with Darwin aboard in December of 1831. The two-year journey stretched to five years, and Darwin spent much of that time taking careful notes of everything he saw at sea and on land. Every day, in his cramped cabin, he wrote in his journal about the landscape—the trees, rivers, and flowers—and the local creatures and people. Occasionally, he sent pages of his journals home to his professor friend, along with his letters. Charles didn't know it at the time, but these pages were sent around to different scientists. When he returned to England in 1836, he was already something of an academic celebrity. The incredible creatures he'd seen on his journey also started him down the path to developing the theory that would transform our understanding of the world—the theory of evolution.

Although Darwin's personality, and his looks, caused the captain to question whether the young scientist was fit for the trip, he turned out to be its most important member. If not for Darwin, that voyage would probably be lost to history. So what if he wasn't the outgoing, seaworthy scientist that FitzRoy would've preferred? Thanks to his acute talents as an observer, and his careful efforts to record all that he saw and to explain it later in books and lectures, Darwin turned the voyage of the *Beagle* into one of the most important expeditions in the history of science. Without him aboard, it would have been just another sailing trip.

UNDERWATER ADVENTURE

This next adventure story definitely goes in the "don't try this at home" category—but it's all true. It's about a teenager named Justin who had been a tinkerer since he was very young. Justin loved building with blocks and creating sculptures from driftwood, and by the time he was ten years old, he had started making his own remote-controlled boats and cars. His parents recognized this passion early on. They'd take him to the local junkyard to pick up old computers, motors, and anything else that Justin found interesting. The manager of the junkyard even started putting interesting items aside for the kid who'd transform those scraps into all kinds of vehicles and robots.

Justin's obsession evolved. He was utterly convinced that he wanted to build a submarine. When he was fourteen years old, he tried to build one, but the walls weren't watertight. He tried again a year later, but the second attempt failed as well. Eventually, Justin decided he was going about it all wrong, and he asked his dad to buy him a six-foot-long, two-foot-wide plastic drainage pipe. By that point, his father had become used to Justin's odd experiments, so after many safety-related questions, he agreed.

When the drainage pipe arrived, Justin dragged it down to his basement, where he stored a vast collection of old electronics, motors, wires, cables, and more, and he started thinking about how to begin. Over the next six months, working entirely on his own, Justin transformed that enormous piece of plastic into a working one-man submarine. He used a motor from an old fishing boat, batteries from toy cars, fins from a run-down Jet Ski, and an air pressure system he had grabbed off a busted soda machine. Friends and family members would occasionally check on his progress and offer to help, but the submarine was a solitary project. When his school was closed due to a heavy snowstorm, he didn't hunt down his friends to hang out. He spent the entire day threading wires from the control panel to the submarine's different components. For him, this was not a chore. It was exactly how he wanted to spend his time.

By the spring, the submarine was finished, and with his parents' permission, Justin steered it into the lake behind their weekend home, ducking below the surface. He was alone underwater for thirty minutes, munching Oreo cookies, looking for fish, and occasionally checking in with his parents over a walkie-talkie to assure them that he was dry.

Toward the end of that dive, he called his dad to inform him that he had a problem. His father panicked until Justin reported the problem: "I'm out of Oreos."

There are a number of reasons this teenager was able to build his own submarine. He was extremely intelligent—but he was also tremendously focused and capable of long, uninterrupted stretches of hard work. Justin spent an entire snow day home from school alone with his wiring! He never felt that his introversion was a character flaw. It was one of his gifts, and when he was working on a submarine or a remote-controlled car, he experienced joy and adventure alike.

DON'T LET FEAR BE A THIEF

Not all adventures have historical or technological impact, and they don't have to. For example, Rita, a once-shy girl in Indiana, spent a year abroad in Ecuador during her sophomore year of high school. There she befriended local kids, learned salsa dancing, and adjusted to a culture that felt warmer, friendlier, and louder than what she was used to. After she returned home, she gave a speech about the study abroad program to encourage other young people to travel as she had. Rita was nervous about speaking in front of everyone, but she believed in her message. Although the adults who ran the exchange program had imagined that extroverted kids would fare better abroad, Rita spoke about how being introverted was actually an enormous advantage. Since she was so comfortable listening— *really* listening—to what people had to say, she formed close friendships with both her host family adults and the kids in her school. Yes, she wore an extroverted mask at times, but Rita didn't feel that she had changed. "I didn't become less introverted," she says. "I just became less shy."

Her high school also asked her to give a speech about her experience. This time, she'd have to speak in front of hundreds of people. Public speaking terrified Rita, but she reasoned that if she could adventure across the world to a place where she didn't speak the language or know anyone and come back speaking Spanish and having made deep new friendships— well, then she could give a quick public speech. She also remembered something one of her neighbors had told her. Before Rita left for Ecuador, her mother had given her a small book filled with handwritten notes of advice from her friends and neighbors. "One of my neighbors wrote, 'Fear is a thief.' And it became my mantra when I was in Ecuador. I decided to live by the words my neighbor shared with me: 'You cannot let fear become a thief. It will steal so many precious things and rob you of so many incredible moments.'"

Rita had heeded that advice as she ventured abroad, and now she turned to it again. She worked with her English teacher to prepare the speech, and then she practiced with the school's theater teacher, making notes about when to speak louder and which words to emphasize. Still, on the morning of the talk, she was overcome with nerves. More than a thousand people were staring back at her. But she glanced at her notes and started to speak. "As soon as I got the first sentence out, everything seemed to just slow down a bit, and I felt calm." Yes, there was a huge crowd sitting out there, but all those people were there for a reason: They were interested in what Rita had to say. This was a chance to share her ideas and experiences and perhaps even inspire other kids to travel and explore new cultures. She was not going to let fear steal that opportunity.

The confidence Rita gained from her adventure carried over into more than just public speaking. She found that it was easier to make new friends now that she'd leaped bigger social hurdles. In fact, she was so changed by the adventure that she decided to delay attending college in favor of taking a gap year and joining another exchange program. This time she headed to Russia. Again, she knew very little about the country. She didn't speak the language and she didn't know a soul there. Russia was even farther from her hometown than Ecuador.

In other words, it was the perfect trip.

THE INTROVERT'S GUIDE TO ADVENTURE

Where and whether you choose to go, or how you choose to get there, is entirely up to you. But if you do embark on an adventure of your own, consider a few tips from the journeys of Jessica, Rita, and the others:

PURSUE YOUR PASSION: The adventurous introverts in this chapter were all so interested in something that they couldn't resist the pull to explore it. Pay attention to what makes you curious, and let it lead you in a direction that might provide a life-changing experience.

LISTEN AND OBSERVE: Whether you're traveling or trailblazing, your strengths as an introvert will suit you well. Rita grew accustomed to Ecuadorian culture by listening closely to her host mother and watching her new classmates. Darwin's powers of observation transformed what would have been a forgettable trip into one of history's great journeys. In this way, introverts are made for adventure.

RECHARGE: No matter how adventurous you are, you're still going to need that time to yourself to recharge your mental batteries. Take Jenny, the swimmer, who also traveled to Japan for several weeks to study the culture. Her host family didn't understand her need to be alone, but she insisted, and they ended up granting her a small block of time after school each day to sit quietly by herself. It made all the difference.

LIVE BY INTROVERT ELEANOR ROOSEVELT'S WORDS: "Do one thing every day that scares you." It can be small, like raising your hand in class, or sitting next to someone you don't know in an assembly. Daring yourself to stretch beyond what's comfortable can be addictive. If you get into the habit, you might soon find yourself doing challenging but rewarding things regularly.

TRUST YOURSELF: Grand journeys, record-breaking expeditions, and even simple foreign travel can be nerve-racking for anyone, extrovert or introvert. But as Rita learned, you can't let fear be a thief.

Chapter Twelve
CHANGING THE WORLD
THE QUIET WAY

Montgomery, Alabama. Early evening on December 1, 1955. A public bus pulls to a stop and a sensibly dressed woman in her forties gets on. She walks tall, despite having spent the day bent over an ironing board in a dingy basement tailor shop at the Montgomery Fair department store. Her feet are swollen, her shoulders ache. She sits in the first row of the "Colored" section and watches quietly as the bus fills with riders. Until the driver orders her to give her seat to a white passenger.

The woman utters a single word that ignites one of the most important civil rights protests of the twentieth century, one word that helps to change America.

The word is *no*.

The driver threatens to have her arrested.

"You may do that," says Rosa Parks.

A police officer arrives. He asks Parks why she wouldn't move.

"Why do you all push us around?" she answers simply.

"I don't know," he says. "But the law is the law, and you're under arrest."

On the afternoon of her trial and conviction for disorderly conduct, the Montgomery Improvement Association holds a rally for Parks at the Holt Street Baptist Church, in the poorest section of town. Five thousand people gather to support Parks's lonely act of courage. They squeeze inside the church until its pews can hold no more. The rest wait patiently outside, listening through loudspeakers. The Reverend Martin Luther King Jr. addresses the crowd. "There comes a time that people get tired of being trampled over by the iron feet of oppression," he tells them.

He praises Parks's bravery and hugs her. She stands silently, her mere presence enough to galvanize the crowd. The association launches a citywide bus boycott that lasts 381 days. People trudge miles to work. They carpool with strangers. They change the course of American history.

I had always imagined Rosa Parks as a stately woman with a bold temperament, someone who could easily stand up to a busload of scowling passengers. But when she died in 2005 at the age of ninety-two, the flood of obituaries recalled her as soft-spoken, sweet, and small in stature. They said she was "timid and shy" but had "the courage of a lion." They were full of phrases like "radical humility" and "quiet fortitude." *What does it mean to be quiet and have fortitude?* these descriptions seemed to ask. *How can you be shy* and *courageous?*

Parks herself seemed aware of this paradox, calling her autobiography *Quiet Strength*—a title that challenges us to question our assumptions. Why *shouldn't* quiet be strong? And what else can quiet do that we don't give it credit for?

As you'll see in this chapter, being quiet can change the world.

THE RUBBER BAND THEORY OF PERSONALITY

A few years ago, I had the chance to meet with one of the leading thinkers in the science of personality, Dr. Carl Schwartz of Harvard Medical School. He explained that our personalities are, to some extent, hardwired into our brains and nervous systems from birth. As we talked about earlier, we are born with temperaments—the tendency to act and feel in specific ways—and we cannot switch our temperaments at will.

Yet we *can* stretch ourselves. The sensitive and cautious can learn to act boldly; the impulsive and outspoken can learn to delay gratification and be diplomatic.

I like to think of this as the rubber band theory of personality. We introverts are able to stretch like rubber bands when we want to, acting outgoing or hanging around in an over-stimulating environment. But if pulled too far, we can snap. The trick is to know our own limits.

One of my favorite rubber band stories involves a former classmate of mine at Princeton University, a woman named Wendy Kopp, who came up with a bold new idea for improving education in America. Schools in the poorest towns struggle to make ends meet. Class sizes are large, and there aren't enough teachers to go around. When Kopp was in college, she suspected that some of her young, smart classmates might be interested in teaching in those neglected towns if given the chance. What the college graduates needed was an organization that would create these opportunities for them. Once Kopp started thinking more about the idea, she realized it could be a way to improve the education of countless kids.

Yet she also knew that she needed money to make it work. And not pocket change, either. After some research, Wendy Kopp figured that her idea, an organization that she'd call Teach for America, would initially require about two and a half million dollars to run properly. She'd need the funds to recruit those young people, train them to be teachers, and pay them for their efforts. But Wendy herself was just a student at the time. She didn't have that kind of money. And she didn't know anyone who did, either, which meant that if she wanted her idea to become a reality, she'd have to ask other people for donations.

For some people, this would have been easy. But Wendy Kopp did not think of herself as the typical outgoing salesperson, capable of charming people into supporting her ideas. She was a proud introvert who cherished solitude. In college, she declined to join the popular social clubs, and enjoyed going on long, solitary runs each morning to clarify her thoughts. I can still remember seeing her walk across campus, long before she created her organization. She had an aura of purpose and determination that I'll never forget. And so Kopp did what many driven, industrious introverts would do in her situation. She headed to the library and immersed herself in research. She studied as much as she could about the problem, and what it would take for her to build her organization.

Then she began writing to the leaders of thirty major companies, including Coca-Cola and Delta Airlines. Most of them rejected her. Some didn't respond at all. But she pressed forward. She graduated from college and, for the rest of the summer, worked alone in a small office writing hundreds of letters. At one point she convinced a fast-talking Texas billionaire named Ross Perot to meet with her privately. Perot fired questions at her, but she calmly answered each one, eventually convincing him that her plan was worthwhile. He was one of her first donors.

Once she was able to raise the rest of the money and launch her organization, Kopp struggled with her responsibilities as a leader of the group. When the first teachers gathered together for a training session at the University of Southern California, she tried to avoid them. When they ate in the cafeteria together, she'd stay in her office. This was equivalent to inviting a few dozen people over to your house for a party and then spending the whole time in your room! The aspiring teachers terrified Wendy. Later, she referred to those eight weeks of training as the longest of her life.

As the years passed, and her organization grew, Kopp learned that she couldn't keep up this way—she had to stretch herself. Even if she didn't love meeting with people, the *cause* needed her. She came down from her office, and instead of avoiding discussions, she started striking them up herself. On most days, she'd be in meetings from nine in the morning until eight o'clock at night—that's a long time for an introvert *or* extrovert! Then she'd go home, sleep for a few hours, and wake up at the crack of dawn. That way, she'd have a few hours to work her favorite way: all alone. The work was exhausting, but her efforts paid off. Teach for America grew to become one of the most important educational institutions in the country.

BOOKS ABROAD

Robin was always hearing the same kind of thing from teachers: "Speak up more in class! Make an effort to socialize with other students!" Truth is, Robin preferred being by herself or with one of her good friends. She especially hated crowds. When she had to give a presentation for school, she never looked up from the floor, since she was terrified that she would start trembling if she caught someone's eye. Small talk bored her. When she hung out with her friends, they had thoughtful conversations about what mattered to them: their families, beliefs, and social lives.

One of Robin's favorite pastimes was reading. She loved to write and play the piano too, but when she needed to recharge, she would usually retreat to her room and disappear into a novel. She liked reading anything from Charles Dickens to John Green. Her best friend was also a bookworm, and their love of literature connected them. They started to brainstorm ways they could share their passion with others. "I thought, 'Why not have a book drive for people who don't get the chance to read?'" Robin recalled. Her friend agreed that this was a great idea, and they set out to decide the best place to donate books to. They wanted to find a charity they really believed in.

At first, they looked at local organizations, but eventually Robin stumbled across the African Library Project, a non-profit group that helps kids run drives for book-hungry schools. To take part, they'd have to collect at least one thousand books and more than five hundred dollars to fund the shipping. The Project selected a destination for them: a library in Malawi, a small, impoverished nation in the southeast corner of Africa.

One of the first people Robin appealed to for help was an older cousin. He was a principal at a nearby school, so she figured he might have some good advice. In the end, not only did he have a few good suggestions, but he even agreed to donate eight hundred books from his school library. He also encouraged Robin to reach out to her own principal for help with the project.

Asking her cousin for help was relatively easy; he was family. But talking to her own school's principal was another challenge entirely. At Robin's school, the students had to wear uniforms nearly every day. In the past, the school had raised money for charities through dress-down days, which meant that students would be allowed to wear what they wanted if they donated ten dollars to the cause. One of these dress-down days would surely raise more than enough money to cover the shipping, but first Robin needed to secure permission from her principal, and talking to him intimidated her. Yet he was her best chance to make the book drive a success.

Robin figured that the more knowledgeable she was about the charity, the more convincing she'd be. She researched the organization and learned all she could about the people she wanted to help, including the literacy rates in the area. She also talked her friend into attending the meeting with her, for support. The principal didn't yell or breathe fire at this shy student, but unfortunately he didn't approve her idea, either. It turns out he didn't like dress-down days and wasn't eager to approve one.

Robin wasn't ready to give up on her project, though. She appealed to the school's community service coordinator, who suggested a few other options. By the end of the week, Robin and her friend had arranged a "penny wars" campaign. They set up two collection bins in the cafeteria, one for girls and one for boys, and challenged their classmates to see which gender could raise more money. Robin's friends spread the word, and they decorated flyers and taped them around the school and the town, requesting money, books, or both. At one point, Robin stood up in front of her brother's Boy Scout troop and spoke to the nearly two dozen boys and their parents. She was nervous, but she tapped into her passion for the project, explaining the low literacy rates in Malawi and how she hoped to help change that. By the end of her talk, the scouts were donating their own allowances.

The books and the money began trickling in. By that summer, after six months of work, Robin and her classmates had collected 1,177 books. She discovered that she'd need about six hundred dollars in shipping costs, and since she was a little short of that, she sold some of the extra books to a used bookstore to make up the difference. Then she gathered a few friends and family members, transformed her house into a mailroom, turned on some music, and the group deftly packed twenty-three enormous boxes of books. There were all kinds of books—children's stories, textbooks, and even a nice atlas.

When Robin finally delivered the boxes to the post office, handing off the fruit of all her labor, she felt an enormous sense of relief. More than anything, though, she felt proud. That pride turned into confidence, both in herself and in her ability to accomplish her goals.

COLLABORATING FOR A CAUSE

As class co-presidents of their Manhattan private school, extroverted Brian and introverted James brought their complementary skills together in order to promote a great cause. (We heard more about their surprisingly well-matched partnership in chapter 8.) During their student council presidency, they introduced a number of fun and educational events such as day trips to amusement parks, assemblies, and talent shows. Perhaps the accomplishment that they were most proud of, though, was expanding the school's community service efforts. Their plan was to encourage kids to get involved in the local food pantry. So the pair organized a school-wide assembly and, in front of seven hundred and fifty kids, described the pantry's work and why they needed help. Brian the extrovert was thrilled to be up on stage. "I was making jokes and having fun," he recalled.

Introverted James? Not so much. But despite his nerves, he spoke too. He explained to his class that the cheapest food is often the least healthful. As a result, people in lower-income neighborhoods in New York City lacked access to the right foods. The pantry they worked with served free, healthy food, James said, but they needed more volunteers.

Thanks to James's quiet passion and Brian's ready charm, nearly three dozen students signed up to volunteer.

MENTORSHIP

As Carly, an introverted musical theater actress, got closer to graduating, she reflected on how she had evolved through the transition from elementary school to middle school, and from middle school to high school. More than anything else, she felt, her high school's community service program helped her grow by realizing that she could be a very generous person.

The school requires students to perform twenty-four hours of community service during junior and senior years. "It's definitely changed me," says Carly. "I volunteer a lot outside the requirements."

Carly volunteered for a local drug-resistance program for children and teenagers in her hometown in Vermont, serving as a counselor for their K–8 after-school and summer programs. Her goal was to provide nonjudgmental support to kids at risk for substance use.

"I was always aware of the kind of stuff that they promote and it feels important. It's powerful because you can be a mentor for kids without them even realizing it. It's fun just working with them and having an impact." The way Carly sees it, being a naturally quiet person is part of what makes her a good volunteer. By patiently listening to the younger kids, she's able to empathize with them.

An introvert herself, Carly makes a particular point to give attention to the quiet kids. "It's a big group, and sometimes we try to put the more shy and introverted kids together when we do group activities, just so they realize there are other kids like them. They're not alone. They have friends. During the summer program we go swimming every day after lunch. It's the fun thing they have to look forward to. They can hang out with friends or on their own. Some kids just play in the sand and read. I totally know where they're coming from, so I don't try to stop them."

SHAKING THE WORLD QUIETLY

In the introvert's manifesto at the start of this book, I quoted Mahatma Gandhi. This slight, peaceful sage, who insisted on nonviolence and restraint, led a revolution that changed the course of history. In 1947, after almost two centuries of oppression, India was at last free from Britain's unjust rule. And it was introverted Gandhi who brought the nation to independence.

You don't have to battle nations to change the world, though. Young people like Robin and Carly show that you can take one small step at a time, and you don't need to be loud or outgoing to achieve your goals. Here are some tips on how to make a difference in your own way:

FIND A POWERFUL CAUSE: Any noble pursuit will test you at times, so you have to be sure to choose something that resonates deeply with you. For Robin, an insatiable reader, this was a library project. For you, it might be something completely different.

USE YOUR STRENGTHS: When Wendy Kopp set out on her quest to improve the nation's poorest schools, she began by researching—which came naturally to her. She immersed herself in the problem, studying everything she could. Embrace *your* quiet strength.

MAKE MEANINGFUL CONNECTIONS: Find people who might want to join your mission. You don't have to know everyone. A few deep, authentically chosen relationships can be more powerful than a whole bunch of superficial ones.

STRETCH YOUR RUBBER BAND: Although you'll need to rely on your strengths as an introvert, there will undoubtedly be times you have to leave your comfort zone. Robin stood in front of the Boy Scout troop. James rallied his classmates to volunteer and donate. Wendy learned to embrace her role as a leader and engage more directly with her staff. It's not always easy—it doesn't have to be—but you can do it!

PERSEVERE: The right cause is going to demand effort and present difficult moments when you're not sure you can go on. Robin had to overcome the disinterested principal at her school. Wendy endured countless rejections as she started her organization. And in an extraordinary feat of bravery, Rosa Parks stood up for an entire community by refusing to kowtow to oppressive laws. These people believed in their missions, so they pushed through—and succeeded.

Chapter Thirteen
QUIET IN THE SPOTLIGHT

Though we might not be the loudest or most attention-seeking, there *are* many young introverts who find ways to perform and share their talents with others. The process of taking the stage is different for everyone. Some introverts are not shy and actually enjoy the spotlight, feeling that their ability to memorize lines and control the interaction is a safe way to connect with an audience. Others *are* shy, except when they're performing a role: "It's not really me that's up there," they say. Others are terrified, but grit their teeth and push themselves forward.

Still others want nothing to do with the stage—and that's okay too. As you know, in my case it took me several decades to grow comfortable giving speeches. For your own comfort, I hope you'll get there more quickly than I did—but you should proceed at your own pace. And in the meantime, I want to introduce you to some young performers whose stories might strike a chord for you.

Carly considers herself pretty introverted, but she's not exactly shy. She's always been highly involved in group extra-curriculars. She joined the school chorus when she was a fresh-man and she even performed at Carnegie Hall and Lincoln Center. She also played team sports year-round throughout high school.

With that chorus background, she landed one of the star-ring roles in her school's spring musical senior year. She'd always felt safe singing in the chorus or playing on a sports field among a team of players, but now she would be reciting a monologue and singing a solo onstage beneath a spotlight! This was a much scarier proposition. But Carly's school had a strong arts program—the director and choreographer of the musical had each trained on Broadway—and she was excited to get feedback on her acting and singing.

There were five performances of the show, and each one sold out. That first night was hectic. To Carly's surprise, though, by drawing on past experience as both a singer and an athlete, she was able not only to do a fantastic job but also to beat her nerves.

"The best advice someone gave me was not to look at the audience. Look at the balcony or the light booth. By the sec-ond performance, I'd gotten over the nervous thing. I think having that background as an athlete helped. Our director kept telling us that sports and theater actually are connected. You have to practice a ton, and in a way, playing a sport in front of an audience is like putting on a show."

Liam is another introvert who loves to perform. He had already established himself as a theater buff in first grade, and every year since, he has nabbed the funny part in the school play. He wouldn't call himself a class clown, though; his comedic skills come through in his acting more than in his day-to-day life. "I'm pretty quiet in general. It's more fun for me to make people laugh in the performances. I don't tell that many jokes when I'm just hanging out or in class." For Liam, being outgoing and funny is easiest when he's in character. It's part of his assignment, and he knows just what to do. Onstage, his role feels clear.

Making conversation in person, offstage, sometimes feels less clear-cut to these young performers. Though he likes most of the kids in his class, Liam prefers to hang out one-on-one with his best friend, Elliot, whom he's known since first grade. They connect through their interest in comedy. When the boys aren't just hanging out and talking, they're making videos using Liam's iPad. Sometimes the boys are the stars of the videos, or sometimes Liam's pets—including two dogs, a turtle, and a cat—are the main attraction.

"We make fake ads, or make up stories. We write some down, but it's mostly improv. Learning about comedy makes me want to get better at it. I like reading books that make me laugh, and I watch movies and skits that are funny that other YouTube users make." The boys have just started posting their videos on YouTube and are excited to get more fans.

Liam found that the positive feedback he gets for his comedic skills, both onstage and online, gave him the confidence to try a totally different performance skill: playing the drums. "I love the drums, but practice is hard work. While I'm playing, it's not always fun. The funnest part for me is hearing how much I improve over time. I'm excited to show everyone how good I'm getting."

Joining the rock band at school and performing at the school's annual music night was the perfect way to do this. All the parents came. Everyone was nervous about messing up, but even if they had, "we were playing too loudly for anyone to notice," Liam said with a grin. Now this actor, comedian, and introvert can add musician to his growing list of identities.

A SHY INTROVERT SHINES

Carly and Liam are examples of introverts who are not especially shy. Though they mostly keep to themselves and their close friends, their introverted nature doesn't get in the way of their ability to be bold in front of others. But Ryan, a boy from Georgia, is both introverted *and* shy. For him, taking the spotlight took years of practice. He dabbled in talent shows, but he never felt good about his performances.

Still, the stage lured Ryan in high school, when he joined the drama club and landed a role in *The Andersonville Trial*, a play set during the Civil War. His nervousness about performing pushed him to deeply research his role. Ryan was cast as an inmate at the Andersonville Prison, a Confederate camp in which 13,000 Union prisoners died. At the first rehearsal, Ryan read his lines without much feeling. Later, though, the club took a field trip to the actual site of the prison. Once he was there, Ryan began to imagine what it must have been like for those prisoners, living in such squalid conditions, with people dying all around them. He dug deeper into the character he was supposed to play, and when he stepped onstage for the actual performance, he was no longer just reciting the words in the script. He'd thought so intently about the situation that he had nearly transformed himself into that prisoner.

Ryan found acting to be easier, in a way, than performing in a talent show. The lights and the stares of the audience were still intimidating, but he'd studied his character so fully that he no longer felt as if he was the one up there on the stage. His *character* was standing in front of all those people, not Ryan himself. His quiet observation and empathy turned out to be the driving forces behind his masterful performance.

THE FAIRY GODMOTHER SINGS SOPRANO

Although we're often nervous when eyes are on us, Ryan, Liam, and Carly are proof that introverts aren't always satisfied staying in the audience. Sometimes we *do* feel the pull of the spotlight, and we want the attention and the applause. Our ability to observe can make for strong performances—

we've noticed what works and what doesn't, and have a sense of how to improve it.

In fact, some of the greatest performers of the last few decades are introverts. As I mentioned earlier, Beyoncé is known as a wildly confident and talented performer, but in interviews she describes herself as a shy, private person. Same goes for Michael Jackson, who was known as the King of Pop. He could moonwalk on a stadium stage in front of more than a hundred thousand people. He also happened to spend the rest of his time at home, with close friends and family. And though standup comedians are known for loud, class-clownish behavior, the comedian and writer Steve Martin has admitted, "I am fundamentally shy and still feel slightly embarrassed at disproportionate attention."

Or take Emma Watson. In the Harry Potter films, she does a very nice impression of an extrovert; her Hermione Granger character is constantly raising her hand and standing up for herself and her friends. Yet Watson identifies as an introvert. "Coming to realize that about myself was very empowering," she said in an interview, "because I had felt like, 'Oh my god, there must be something wrong with me, because I don't want to go out and do what all my friends want to do.'

"If I have to be in the public eye," Watson added, "I want it to be for something that was worth it." It makes sense, then, that in 2014 she took on the role of Goodwill Ambassador for UN Women, appearing fearless and poised in a speech at the UN advocating for gender equality.

The very idea of a *performing introvert* might seem like a contradiction, but pediatrician Marianne Kuzujanakis says that performing is not so much a choice as a necessity for introverted actors, musicians, or comedians. "Whether they sing or dance or act, they possess a skill and passion that cries out to be expressed. If being in the public eye is the best way to express their soul, some decide the feeling of risk is well worth it. After their performance, they can again revert to their real selves and re-energize in solitude if need be."

A NUDGE FROM MOM

A fourteen-year-old girl named Victoria had always loved to sing. Victoria was smart, studious, and reserved. She often tried out for school musicals, but never for one of the leading roles. The spotlight didn't attract her in quite the same way it did Ryan; she preferred to blend into the chorus. "I made sure I was behind people," said Victoria.

Then she was faced with a serious challenge.

Victoria's mom had an important meeting on the day of the musical. She promised she would skip the meeting and attend, under one condition: If and only if Victoria landed a leading role. Her mother was tired of trying to pick her daughter's voice out of the chorus. She wanted Victoria to know that she believed in her, and she wanted to see Victoria believe in herself enough to show off her talents.

Victoria decided to give it a try. "I wanted to show people that I did have some musical talents," she recalled. The musical, Stephen Sondheim's *Into the Woods*, offered a number of great roles, and since Victoria wasn't quite ready for the lead, she tried out for the part of Cinderella's fairy godmother. To her surprise, she won the part—and the nerves set in immediately. She'd have to sing soprano, which was several notes above her range. And the script called for her to be dangling six feet above the stage at one point! It was *definitely* not the chorus.

As with the other kids we've met, though, Victoria's introverted side allowed her to excel. While Ryan turned his contemplative approach into an advantage by digging deeper into the character he was playing, Victoria made a strength of her ability to practice and concentrate. She trained for months to reach new heights with her voice, and to prepare for the moment when all eyes and ears in the audience would focus entirely on her. "The whole week before, I was worried I was going to mess up and be all shaky and quivery," she said.

Instead, she found that it felt wonderful to be one of the stars. Just getting hooked up to the microphone was exciting. And despite her fears, everything went perfectly. "When I got onstage, nothing happened. I was completely calm."

With her mother sitting proudly in the audience, Victoria hit all her notes and played the role to perfection. Her mother heard boys and girls in the audience reacting with amazement. "She can sing!" they said. "Who knew?"

FREE TRAIT THEORY

As a research psychologist, Dr. Brian Little is dedicated to studying the complicated ways that the human mind and emotions work. When I met him a few years ago, he was on the faculty at Harvard and one of the most beloved professors on campus. He was known as a passionate and uniquely caring teacher. In college, professors have "office hours" during which students can drop in and speak privately about class or personal matters. When Brian Little held his office hours, the line would stretch out into the hallway, as if he were giving out free Super Bowl tickets.

When he was standing in front of his students, Little would act as outgoing as an extrovert. In private, though, he was introverted and liked time to himself. Is it possible to do both, while staying true to yourself and your quiet strengths? I think you'll find that the answer is yes—as long as you stretch beyond your comfort zone in the service of people or projects you truly care about.

Based on his own experiences, Brian Little came up with a new theory of psychology, known as "Free Trait Theory," to demonstrate this truth. According to Free Trait Theory, we are born with certain personality traits, but we can also adopt new ones when we really need them, in the service of our "core personal projects." So, extroverts aren't the only ones who can turn on the charm onstage. And introverts aren't the only ones who can sit quietly and devour articles online, or spend hours alone practicing an instrument.

Let's go back to Hermione Granger, the extroverted character played by introverted Emma Watson. Hermione's urgent need to talk in class in the Harry Potter novels seems to contrast with her ability to swallow up books, but when she's studying, she's exemplifying Free Trait Theory. Driven by a passion for knowledge, she sits by herself and reads voraciously. Little's theory applies to all of us, and it says that we can take on opposite traits when we're so inspired.

My own history with the spotlight is an example of Free Trait Theory. Today I regularly speak on stages before crowds of hundreds, sometimes thousands, of people. I smile and move and gesticulate to make my points, and I speak with all the energy and passion in my soul. It may sound surprising to speak in front of a huge crowd about introversion, and I could see how someone watching me speak might assume I'm extroverted. I seem comfortable onstage. Sometimes I make people laugh, which feels great. But the reason I'm able to act this way is that I care deeply about what I'm saying. I'm passionate about quiet kids and adults and the fact that we need to be recognized. Talking about it makes me light up!

Needless to say, I wasn't always as comfortable in the spotlight as I am now. I will never forget being in eighth grade, when I was in an English class with some of my good friends. I was surrounded by familiar faces, so I was more at ease than usual and I spoke up more in class. As a result, my teacher had no idea I was shy. We were studying Shakespeare's *Macbeth* one day when she called me up to the front of the room, along with a friend of mine. I immediately went into panic mode—especially when the teacher explained that we were going to perform a sketch, and that my role was Lady Macbeth. My friend was to be the title character, the doomed king of Scotland, and our task was to act out one of the critical scenes. Yet we were not going to read from our books. Instead, she wanted us to improvise our own versions of the lines.

This was supposed to be fun. *Fun?* If I could have disappeared into thin air, I would have. My face turned red. I couldn't open my mouth. I started shaking and, to my teacher's surprise, I had to sit down. I didn't say another word for the rest of the class, and I walked through the halls that day feeling utterly ashamed that I hadn't been able to just get up there and not care.

My teacher was wonderful, and with any other student, that assignment might have been a fantastic experiment. But I had turned the pressure up so high that it felt like a life or death situation.

Today, I know that it's possible to overcome these almost allergic reactions to the spotlight. I even know that my introverted nature can be an *advantage* onstage. I just wish I had known it back then, and hope to save you the same trouble!

AN AUDIENCE OF DOLLS

To a ten-year-old girl named Caitlin, the idea of speaking in front of a group was terrifying. Caitlin was extremely shy and introverted. Her voice was so faint that even her family struggled to hear her, and there were some people she didn't speak to at all. In second grade, her teacher was so frustrated with Caitlin's reluctance to talk that the school recommended she be placed in special education classes. But Caitlin wasn't falling behind. In fact, she was earning high marks in every subject. She was just really, really quiet.

In fifth grade, each student in Caitlin's class was assigned to give a five-minute oral report. Caitlin was nervous, so she began preparing immediately. First she read as much as she could about her chosen subject, Amelia Earhart. Then, once she had become an expert, she made a PowerPoint presentation full of notes about the brave pilot's life. When the presentation was ready, her father joined in. Like Caitlin, he was an introvert, but he had learned to disguise this side of himself when necessary. He had mastered the art of small talk and had become a dedicated member of Toastmasters, an organization that helps adults speak in front of large groups. Now he was passing all of his tricks on to his daughter.

They set up the presentation on his laptop, right in the middle of the living room. First, her father sat in front of her and she spoke only to him, telling the story of Amelia Earhart's life. Next, he propped up ten stuffed animals around the room. He explained that they were stand-ins for the students in her class. Caitlin laughed at how silly and childish that seemed, but he assured her that it was serious. He asked her to try the presentation again, only this time he wanted her to make eye contact with each of those plush figures. This way, when she was actually giving the presentation, she would be accustomed to moving her gaze around the room, only she'd be glancing at her teacher and classmates instead of her stuffed toys. Caitlin and her father practiced that five-minute speech in front of the make-believe audience for more than an hour—that's twelve times! A few days later, she delivered a stellar presentation in class without a glitch, and earned a high grade on the report.

Caitlin's story highlights one of the first clues to thriving in the spotlight: Preparation is absolutely essential. I didn't have the chance to prepare for my Shakespearean improv assignment that day in eighth grade, but later I learned that practice can ready you for anything.

In 2012, I was invited to speak to an audience of 1,500 people at the big TED conference in California. At first I was terrified, but by the date of the talk I'd been training myself to be a better public speaker for almost a year. Like Caitlin's father, I joined Toastmasters. (Later, they honored me with a public speaking award!) I worked with TED's speaking coach. I even met with my own personal acting coach, to help me feel more confident about expressing myself. He taught me about how body language, inflection, and even props can help bring a talk to life.

When it came time to deliver the speech, I was still nervous. Out there in the crowd were Microsoft founder Bill Gates, former vice president Al Gore, and actress Cameron Diaz. But I was ready, and the performance came off beautifully. The experience was a blur, but I've been told that I received a standing ovation, and within a week, my talk had been viewed online over a million times. The lesson here is simple, and it applies to plays, talent shows, and presentations in fifth-grade classrooms just as much as to speeches at conferences. I didn't succeed because I was a natural. I succeeded because I was prepared—and I was prepared because, as an introvert, I *had* to be.

HOW TO SHINE IN THE SPOTLIGHT

The next time you have to perform for an audience, keep these tips in mind. Don't worry about whether you'll *survive* the spotlight. If you follow these steps, you're going to *shine*.

PREPARE: The more work you do beforehand to hone your performance or presentation, the more confident you'll be in front of your audience. First, master the content. Then start practicing. Test your speech or act in front of the mirror, or make a video of yourself and play it back to see how you're coming across. Usually you'll find that you sound and look much better than you think—and this knowledge will make you feel much better.

STUDY THE EXPERTS: If possible, look online for examples of skilled performers in action. Try to find ones who have a similar personal style to yours. Study them. Watch how they stand, move, and alter their voices. But don't try to be something you're not. If you have a great sense of humor, use that. But if you're more serious, there's no need to turn yourself into a comedian; focus on sharing seriously interesting stories. The key to compelling speaking is being wholly yourself onstage—and having something real to say.

SLOWLY BUILD THE PRESSURE: Start practicing by yourself first, then graduate to a few friends or family members. Each time, ask yourself how anxious you are on a scale of 1 to 10. You should be practicing in the 4 to 6 range, not the 7 to 10 range. If that means testing your speech in front of a stuffed animal instead of a group of people, that's just fine.

FAMILIARIZE YOURSELF: If possible, visit the space in which you'll be performing beforehand, whether it's an auditorium, a classroom, or a new and unfamiliar space. Visualize the crowd. Imagine what it will feel like to have a dozen or even hundreds of eyes on you. If that feels unnerving, try to practice in front of a safe and supportive group of friends or family.

BREATHE: When your moment arrives, take a deep breath before you start, and continue to steal deep, relaxing breaths as you speak, sing, or perform. Suck the air in slowly and deeply, so that it expands your stomach like a balloon. When you exhale, that balloon should deflate. Breathe in through your nose, hold it for as long as feels comfortable, and then let it out through your mouth. This advice might sound corny, but it works!

SMILE: This is one of the simplest but most important tricks. Smiling is a great icebreaker. No matter how nervous or uncomfortable you are, smile at your audience before you start. Remind yourself to smile while you're speaking, and do it again at the end. This will make you feel more relaxed and confident, and will likely provoke an ego-boosting return smile from someone in the audience.

CONNECT: Establish eye contact with a few friendly members of the audience throughout your presentation. If someone is grimacing or yawning, look away and find a more energetic, engaged member of the audience. Locking eyes with someone who appears to be interested in your speech will do wonders for your confidence.

LOOK OUTWARD: Leading isn't just about you—it's about the people you're leading. Ask yourself, who are they? How can you best serve them? How can you best teach, help, or make them feel comfortable? Remember that they're there not to judge you. They're there to learn from you. Think of yourself as a role model who can help them, and introduce them to new ideas!

PART FOUR
HOME

Chapter Fourteen
THE RESTORATIVE NICHE

A bedroom. A terrace. A basketball court. A nook in the library. A treehouse from elementary school. A friend's basement. These are all examples people give of their safe spaces—calm retreats for relaxing and recharging. Another term for this safe space is the "restorative niche."

Do you remember building secret forts as a kid? Sometimes they'd be made out of pillows and sheets, other times they'd be high up in trees. A restorative niche is basically the same thing. Find yours! It doesn't have to be secret or a fort, but it should give you a feeling of safety, comfort, and of personal space. The restorative niche can be as small and nearby as a chair in your bedroom, or as wide and majestic as a sandy beach—or anything in between.

The term "restorative niche" was coined by Brian Little, the Harvard psychologist we met in the last chapter. He uses it to describe a physical or even a mental place that allows you to shut out the noise and chaos of the world, to be alone with your thoughts and feelings, and to rejuvenate after a long day of being around people. A restorative niche allows you to return to your true self. As we've already discussed, introverts can be extremely sensitive to outside stimulation. A restorative niche gives us an opportunity to find our optimal zone of stimulation—and our energy. Going to this place is like pressing our restart button.

BATHED IN CHRISTMAS LIGHTS

A few years ago, I visited a school in Ohio to talk about the power of introverts. A student named Gail had started to see herself in some of the stories I told. In learning more about introversion, Gail began to understand why she was often uncomfortable in supposedly fun environments, and at peace with herself when she was alone or with just a few friends. The concept of a restorative niche ignited a spark in Gail.

She realized that she didn't have any place like this in her life. At home, she spent most of her time in the living room, but the television would usually be on, and it distracted her from daydreaming, reading, or doing her homework. She had her own bedroom, but it was dark and gloomy. Oh, and it was also a total mess.

After Gail heard about the idea of a restorative niche, she decided to make some changes. If her room was going to be her sanctuary, the place where she could press reset and return to her true self, then she needed it to have a little more cheer. After she hung up her clothes and threw out some old papers, she tackled the lighting problem. She pinned the family's old Christmas lights to her bedroom ceiling so that they stretched across the room, and plugged them into the outlet in the corner. It was such a simple change, but it gave her room a cool, moody glow. Gail was thrilled.

Lola's niche is also her bedroom. "I love to entertain myself. I watch weird documentaries on Netflix or I'll pick a director and just watch a bunch of their movies. I like to research random facts, and find out about things. I need space to unwind and recharge. It's necessary. You're not going to leave your house without your phone charged—that's how I feel about *myself*."

These niches can change with the seasons too. During the wintertime, Lola hibernates in her room. In the summer, her niche is the skate park, or the fire escape with a smoothie and a book.

THE RESTORATIVE STALL

Brian Little himself often takes advantage of restorative niches. Although he regularly delivers rousing speeches (which usually end in standing ovations), he found that acting like an extrovert was completely exhausting. After his funny, insightful performances for delighted crowds of students and executives, he often needs to retreat to a peaceful spot for some alone time.

Years ago, Little was asked to deliver a speech at the Royal Military College Saint-Jean near Montreal, Canada. The school is located on the banks of the Richelieu River. Little's speech was a huge success and his hosts asked if he would join them for lunch afterward. He didn't want to be rude, but he also knew that he needed some time alone to recharge after all that talking. So he fibbed, informing his hosts that he had a passion for boats and that he hoped they wouldn't mind if he spent his lunch hour walking along the river. They obliged and, thankfully, not one of them shared this make-believe passion, so they left him alone to stroll. When he returned after lunch, he was once again ready to talk.

Little was such a success that the school continued to invite him back annually. Each year, he used that stroll along the river to recuperate between talks. Then the college moved to an urban location. Little returned for another speech, but he no longer had his river. So, instead, he snuck away to the restroom during lunch. That's right: He found it more relaxing to sit in a bathroom stall than to join his colleagues for lunch. At times he even lifted his feet up so that no one would recognize his shoes and try to strike up a conversation through the door.

Restorative niches are essential to an introvert's happiness. We love our downtime after a long day of school, family, and friends. Unfortunately, though, it's not always easy for kids and teens to seek solitude. Think back to the story of Lucy.

When she was exhausted from acting outgoing all morning and tried to eat lunch by herself, her friends confronted her. They thought she was mad at them and couldn't understand why she wanted to be alone. And according to recent scientific research, their reaction probably wasn't all that unusual. A preference for solitude often clashes with middle-school social norms that emphasize cliques and crowds. In one study, researchers questioned 234 eighth graders and about 200 high school seniors. The scientists found that a desire for solitude was frowned upon among the middle-school kids, while the high school seniors were much more accepting.

Granted, there's an important difference between a healthy, restorative break from others and antisocial behavior. Some of the kids in the research study preferred solitude because they lacked the social skills to engage with their peers, and I've heard from kids who had similar struggles. When Bailey was in middle school, she'd eat lunch in a bathroom stall every day, all by herself. This wasn't exactly the kind of break that Brian Little recommends. Bailey was hiding. The cafeteria, the cliques, and the stares of her classmates were all too much for her to handle. Eventually, she became so overwhelmed that she couldn't bear being in school and left for a while. Thankfully, Bailey ultimately faced her fear. With practice, she developed the skills to care for herself while engaging in her surroundings. But it's important to understand the distinction here. When I suggest seeking out a restorative niche,

I'm not recommending a place to hide (though of course we all need to hide sometimes). It should be a place to take a breath, unwind, and recharge so that you can face the normal pressures of the day.

The easiest place to carve out your spot might very well be at home. In school, withdrawal has social costs, but at home, as long as you explain your need for solitude, you can often be left in peace, without fear of judgment. (We'll talk more about home life and family in the next chapter.)

Cultivating the right niche can have other benefits beyond relaxation and rejuvenation. Remember that lemon juice study? The experiment showed how introverts are more sensitive to external stimulation, and the scientist behind the study, Hans Eysenck, also believed that we have ideal levels of stimulation. So, extroverts might seek out noise and crowds, but introverts look for peace and privacy. We don't do this simply to relax. It also helps us think clearly.

In another famous study, introverts and extroverts were asked to play a difficult word game while wearing headphones that emitted random bursts of noise. When the participants in the study were allowed to choose the volume of those noises, the introverts opted for a lower decibel level than the extroverts. Both groups performed well. (This reinforces the idea that neither personality type is better or smarter. We're just different and sensitive to different things.) Yet when the volume on the introverts' headsets was turned up, and that of the extroverts' lowered, both groups performed worse than they had previously.

This suggests that we all have our own ideal level of stimulation, a kind of sweet spot that combines the right music, the perfect volume, even the ideal lighting, temperature, and crowd. And when we find that sweet spot, we can be mentally sharper and potentially happier.

FORTRESS OF SOLITUDE

Even superheroes need a restorative niche. Consider Batman, the caped crime fighter. After a long night of battling nefarious villains, he retreats to his Batcave, a cavernous underground lair. He could slip into any of Wayne Manor's many rooms and close the door, but for him, the Batcave is where he can truly be himself. And he's not the only superhero with a restful lair. Superman too feels the need to retreat. When the pressures of being an alien entrusted with the safety of the human race become too great, he flies up to his own private ice cave, the Fortress of Solitude.

Since the rest of us don't fly or own a Batmobile, we have to create our Fortresses of Solitude at home, or somewhere else that feels safe and cozy. For example, Rupal, the introverted sister of Raj, the mathematician we met in chapter 5, would head right for her room after school and stay there for an hour, listening to music, reading, or doing homework. Her mom would be itching to find out about Rupal's day, but she understood that this time alone was important to her daughter. Rupal needed that recovery period, and usually she would emerge an hour later from her room, content and ready to chat.

Her brother Raj took another approach. He liked to chill out after school too, but didn't need to be alone to do it. He would sit at the kitchen counter and quietly immerse himself in a book or a game. He didn't talk much, and his mother knew better than to bother him. This was his restorative niche. It just so happened that he didn't always like to be alone, so his niche was a few seats away from his mom.

Your choice of a sanctuary depends both on your living space and your unique needs. For Tyler, a seventh grader in Minnesota, any outdoor space does the trick, as long as he's surrounded by trees. Nature makes him feel calm and steady. As an introverted kid at a crowded school, his two favorite hobbies are ones that not only allow him but actually *require* him to be quiet: fishing and hunting. "In the summer, my dad, my grandma, and I will go out early morning to hike and catch ducks, or we'll take out the boat and fish. You need concentration, bug spray, and total silence." The woods and the lake, he says, with their wide space and clean air, make all the stress of friends and studying fall away.

His second-favorite place to unwind: in midair. That's because Tyler is lucky to have a big backyard with a trampoline in it. When he needs to blow off steam, jumping up and down and looking at the horizon is another way to just breathe in the fresh air.

Meanwhile, Rita, the world traveler, considers the back porch of her family home to be a perfect restorative spot. She doesn't need solitude; she sits together with her whole family. Sometimes they talk, but often they'll just listen to the birds or the sound of the wind blowing through the trees.

Throughout high school, Noah found that his restorative niche was playing video games in his basement. His parents wondered why he loved gaming so much. They worried that it was an escape from real life. But for Noah, the stories in the games were inspiring. He found that they sparked his creativity in more ways than just wanting to be a better gamer: They made him excited to create new stories, and to illustrate them.

Hanging out in a restorative niche is about relaxing; it's about exploring your interests; but most of all it's about being yourself.

RESTORATIVE HEADPHONES

What if you don't have any privacy or peace in your own home? Privacy is very important to Karinah, especially as someone who shares a room with her older sister, with no lock on the door. Karinah finds solitude by writing short stories while listening to music on her headphones. When her sister is being loud or taking up space, Karinah goes on the back porch to read. If no one's in the kitchen, she'll bake brownies while streaming a TV show from her laptop.

And if she can't find any quiet spot, Karinah creates one in her mind. "I think tuning out sound and people is something I do subconsciously. Nobody else can go in there. That feels safe."

When you can't get away to your restorative niche, consider bringing restorative things with you! Some kids even manage to find peace while packed into a crowded school bus. Julie, a teenager from New Jersey, said many people assumed she wasn't "a morning person" because she seemed grumpy on the bus ride to school. She'd climb on and not talk to a soul, but she wasn't moody or trying to be rude. Julie just needed time to herself after she woke up, to prepare for the chaos of the day. So she'd find a window seat, pop in her earphones, listen to music, and stare out at the passing cars, trees, and buildings as the bus rolled along. There were kids all around her, but— like Davis with his earplugs—she was in her peaceful place inside her head, getting ready for the day.

HOW TO CREATE A RESTORATIVE NICHE

You can escape into your room, like Gail, or into a book or a song you're writing, or even into a bathroom stall, like Dr. Little. We all need these quiet, restorative times in our day, and if you've already found that spot in your life, embrace it.

If you haven't, here are a few suggestions for carving out your own little niche:

THE BEDROOM SANCTUARY: Your own room is often the best spot for retreating to recharge. Consider simple changes that will make your bedroom cozier, as Gail did with her cleaning campaign and holiday lights.

A QUIET CORNER: Sometimes you don't have the luxury of your own room at home. Or you might need to recharge in the middle of the day at your crowded school. In that case, find a peaceful spot in a corner, sit down, open a book, listen to music, or just close your eyes and breathe.

NATURE: Trees can be great retreats, since they offer physical distance between you and the crowd, and their presence is naturally soothing. Or consider Brian Little's technique: Simply walking around outside, even circling the courtyard or playground of your school, can be a great way to relax.

YOUR OWN HEAD: When you're stuck in a crowd—on the bus, in the cafeteria, or in a house packed with brothers and sisters—you can create your own sanctuary in your mind, aided by a pair of headphones, a book, or just by closing your eyes and focusing on your breath.

THE RIGHT ACTIVITY: Doing something that relaxes you can also take the place of a restorative niche. Whether it's playing a video game, jumping on a trampoline, taking a shower, or cooking, find the time to do it. (Also make sure to eat well and to sleep at least eight hours. That goes for extroverts too!)

THE LIBRARY: It's free and it's the perfect place to relax and surround yourself with books for company.

OUTSIDE THE DOOR: If you're feeling overwhelmed in a group, or if you haven't had a private moment in a while, step outside for a minute. When in doubt, go to the restroom. Anywhere you can collect yourself and take a deep breath works.

FIND YOUR FORTRESS OF SOLITUDE

blanket fort

great wall of books

cardboard box barracks

attic lookout

tree branch tower

bathroom stall bunker

abandoned phone booth hideout

top secret headquarters

above the commotion and away from it all

Chapter Fifteen
QUIET WITH FAMILY

Jenny, the shy swimmer you met earlier, had an unusually busy few weeks one summer. First, her family spent a weekend away at a friend's birthday party. The weekend was intensely social, crowded with people who asked Jenny all kinds of questions. "She kept saying that she wanted a break from people," her mother recalled. "She wanted a day of downtime." Yet she already had plans. The morning after returning from the party, Jenny headed out for a week-long sleep-away camp. This wasn't the sort of rowdy, cheering-heavy camp I attended when I was young, but it was close. The camp was filled with driven, extroverted kids, and Jenny did her best to pretend that she was naturally outgoing and outspoken, just to fit in. When she returned home, her family was desperate to hear all about the camp. "We hadn't seen her for a week," her mom recalled. "We were very excited to hear about everything and talk."

Her parents had planned a family dinner, and then a movie

they could all watch together. Unfortunately, another group activity was the last thing Jenny needed. "She was really craving her alone time, but we delayed too long," her mother said. "That night she kind of flipped out."

It was one of those yelling, screaming, door-slamming eruptions—maybe you're familiar with them. These eruptions are not always a bad thing. Introverts can be so bottled up that letting our feelings out with a good freak-out session now and then can actually feel pretty good. It's a huge release, like deflating a balloon.

Yet Jenny and her mother both knew that this particular flipout could have been avoided. Her mother talked to her about it soon after, acknowledging to Jenny that "when you need to recharge your batteries, you *need* to recharge your batteries." Her mother promised that she would try to be better at recognizing when Jenny was reaching her limit, and she asked Jenny to do a better job of expressing it before it became an issue.

It takes a lot of self-awareness to notice these kinds of habits and emotions. Jenny was in her early teens, and her mother felt that it was time she started accepting more responsibility. She knew her daughter was capable of that level of maturity. If Jenny could recognize her needs, then she could express them, retreat to her Fortress of Solitude, relax in that space, and emerge refreshed and tantrum-free. Sounds simple enough, right? Well, there's one more factor: Jenny is part of a family. And when you are part of a family, there are many other needs and feelings to take into account, not merely your own. In particular, Jenny has a sister. And her little sister is her complete opposite.

SCRATCHING AT THE DOOR

Jenny's mother recognized early on that although her daughters were only two years apart, their personalities were *light-years* apart. "Jenny is a cat and Amy is a dog," their mother explained. "Jenny wants to curl up somewhere with a book and be by herself, and Amy is like a puppy. She likes to have a lot of activity around her." Amy always wanted to be around people. Especially her big sister, Jenny.

Whenever Jenny would retreat to her room, hoping to decompress and be alone, her little sister would bang on the door a few minutes later. Jenny would try to be a good older sister, but this could be a challenge. "It really depends on the type of mood I'm in," she said. "If I've hung out with people all day, I'll usually be less prone to say, 'Okay, let's do something together.'" Given that she was a teenager, mood was a strong factor as well. Sometimes she simply didn't feel like obliging her little sister.

The question for Jenny, Amy, and their parents was how to give both girls what they needed. This problem came to a head during one of the family's vacations. They drove up to the Columbia River Gorge, a mountainous paradise that winds through Oregon into Washington. It rained the whole time, which put a damper on the family's plan to swim, sail, kayak, water-ski, and hike. Jenny didn't entirely mind. She had brought books and her sketchpad. She was happy to spend the time reading and drawing in their rented room. For Amy, on the other hand, the weather was a terrible drag.

Eventually, they came to an agreement. Jenny was allowed a certain amount of time to read, and during those periods, Amy had to leave her alone. But then Amy got her time too. Jenny promised to swim in the rain with her sister—and to do it with a smile on her face, not a reluctant scowl. The pair survived the rained-out trip, and the following year their parents stumbled upon a new strategy. They invited one of Jenny's good friends, who happened to be extroverted, and that friend ended up helping satisfy Amy's need for interaction, which allowed Jenny more time to herself. "Throwing somebody else into the mix took some of the pressure off Jenny," her mother said. To her surprise, instead of detracting from the sisters' time together, that extra person actually helped them get along.

OPEN-DOOR POLICY

As I mentioned earlier, I grew up in a family of quiet, contemplative types. Each of us tended toward the introverted end of the spectrum, and I've learned of many other families built the same way. Twin sisters Sophie and Bella thrived at home in part because everyone in the house was introverted, and preferred the quiet. "We all have slower heartbeats around here," their mother, Amanda, said.

The Carver house was very different. Their family was split directly down the middle of the personality divide. Suzanne, the mother, and one of her daughters were both extroverts, while her husband and their other daughter were introverts. Like Jenny's family, the Carvers have struggled with balancing the needs of these differing personalities—even the parents. When her husband turned quiet, Suzanne used to worry that he was upset. While Suzanne was always happy to be talkative, her husband needed those quiet, reflective periods. Their older daughter, Maria, was the same way as their father, while their younger daughter, Gabi, was chatty like their mother, always looking for stimulation, play, and conversation.

One of the ways the family tried to make it work was through an open-door policy. In most cases, the rule in the house was that you could not shut your door and close out the other members of the family. This applied to everyone. But there was one important condition. "You get to describe the parameters of what happens in your room," Suzanne explained. "So if you're reading quietly, someone else can come in and read quietly too, but they can't come in and turn on music and start to dance." This allowed Maria—and her dad—to benefit from necessary quiet time, but it also taught her little sister an important lesson. "One of the things we're trying to teach Gabi is that being in a relationship doesn't mean incessantly talking." Simply being with someone, sitting near them in their room, also counts as quality time.

CATS AND DOGS PLAYING NICELY

So, how can introverts live happily ever after with their families? The stories of Jenny, Maria, and others reveal that it doesn't always come easily, or naturally. But it can be done, as long as you follow these important tips:

COMMUNICATE: Closing your door is okay now and then, but in a family, you have to make sure that in doing so, you're not hurting your loved ones. That goes for annoying little brothers and sisters too. As she matured, Jenny learned how to tell her parents and her sister when she needed alone time.

RESPECT YOUR FAMILY MEMBERS' NEEDS: Just as we introverts want others to respect our need for quiet and solitude, we have to understand that our siblings or parents might have an opposite requirement. We might have to force ourselves to chat when we don't want to. Everyone in the house has an equal right to have their needs met, and that means . . .

COMPROMISE: No matter how much you have in common with each other, there will surely be plenty of ways in which you and a family member differ. Learning to find the right balance between your own desires and those of your sibling or parent is a key to achieving happiness at home. Life within a family—and everywhere—is a process of give and take.

APPRECIATE THE TOGETHER TIME: Your family members are usually the ones you can be your truest self with, and the value of that comfort is enormous. Make sure you're allowing yourself this time when you can be fully yourself. (You can always return to your other sources of entertainment. They're not going anywhere.)

SEEK OUT FAMILY ALLIES: If your parents or siblings aren't understanding where you're coming from, stay in touch with cousins, grandparents, or family friends—other people close to you who care deeply about you and can empathize and offer suggestions.

LIGHTEN YOUR LOAD: A lot of us introverts are drawn to coping with challenges privately. Seek your family's support, reassurance, and love when you're having a hard time. Ask for help or a hug when you need it. That's what family's for!

CONCLUSION

When I was young, I had never heard of the terms *intro-vert* and *extrovert*. But I wish I'd known about the science and psychology of personality, so I could have understood that what I was experiencing was normal. Understanding at a deep level who you are, and what you need, is so empowering. I've experienced it in my own life, as I've matured from a shy girl who struggled with public speaking to a successful author and businesswoman who lectures in stadiums. The process of researching this book, and hearing the stories of so many young people, has only affirmed my belief in the importance of self-awareness. Whether you're an introvert or an extrovert, I hope the stories and insights in this book will help you understand yourself, your friends, your families, and even those random classmates you pass each day in the halls.

While researching this book, my colleagues and I spoke to many inspiring kids and teenagers who reflected on their experiences. One was Ryan, whom you'll remember as the shy actor from chapter 13. He shared a number of stories about his experiences as a performer, but he also sent us an essay he wrote about how understanding introversion has changed his life. The essay is a remarkably mature meditation on what it's like to be a quiet teen, and so I'd like to share its ending here. "I now feel no qualms accommodating my introversion," Ryan wrote. "It isn't a secret to be covered up or a blemish to hide. I don't hold myself to the extrovert ideal anymore, and it is more freeing than I ever could have imagined."

Peter, the Ohio student who used to have a smoking problem, told us: "I'm used to spending time alone; I'm not ashamed of it. I think it's actually prepared me for a lot of social situations. A lot of my friends won't go to a party unless they definitely know someone there, but I don't mind either way. I know how to manage on my own and I feel confident about my ability to occupy and entertain myself." I'm happy to tell you that he doesn't feel the need to leave parties for smoking breaks anymore.

Lola, the popular introvert, echoed this sentiment. "There are times when I wish I were more social, and I want to be like other people. At the same time, I'd rather accept myself as I'm transitioning and not worry how other people are flourishing in their own social lives. I just want to keep accepting myself as how I am."

Whether you're an introvert or an extrovert, I hope this book has opened your eyes and your heart. Here are a few key points to remember as you continue your journey through school and life:

EMBRACE YOUR SUPERPOWER: During your school years, when being loud and social is often such an important social currency, quiet can seem like a weakness. But I hope you now understand that we introverts are a truly powerful bunch. You can count celebrity actresses, revolutionary scientists, brilliant writers, billionaires, All-Star athletes, comedians, and so many other unique individuals as part of your psychological tribe. All of these people, and so many of the kids whose stories I've told in this book, have learned to embrace their secret strengths as introverts: deep thinking, intense focus, comfort with solitude, and excellent listening skills.

EXPAND YOUR COMFORT ZONE: Never use introversion as an excuse to avoid trying something new. I wouldn't have dreamed that I'd become a celebrated public speaker when I was in middle school. But I slowly tested the edges of my comfort zone, practicing in small groups first, then graduating to larger and larger audiences. No matter what you're trying to do, I encourage you to find your own limits and then stretch them, within reason. Stretch your internal rubber band, but do so comfortably.

FIND THE RIGHT LIGHTING: Some of you might thrive in the warm glare of the spotlight. You might truly find yourself onstage, singing, dancing, or inhabiting a character. For others, the right lighting could be the glow of your laptop while you learn code or a single lamp that allows you to read or write in solitude. You have to find what's comfortable for you. Find your fascination—the thing that lights *you* up.

PURSUE THOSE PASSIONS: Nothing motivates you to push yourself and test your limits like a cause, a goal, or an interest. This could be a sport, an art, or an innate desire to tinker and build. Several years ago I learned that my mission was writing, and spreading the Quiet Revolution. I haven't traveled all over the world speaking before huge audiences because I love the attention. The reason I walk out there in front of all those people is that I believe in my mission; I need to tell people about the power of quiet. Find your own passion, remain true to yourself and your strengths, and you will accomplish your goals.

RECHARGE YOUR BATTERIES: As you venture out and test yourself in more extrovert-friendly situations and environments, remember your need for calm and quiet. Take the time to reenergize yourself and find your own restorative niche. It could be a walk along a river, a stretch of time behind a closed door, or even a few minutes with your eyes closed and your headphones on, listening to music as you block out the rest of the world. Electronics don't run well when their batteries are drained. Neither do you.

VALUE TRUE FRIENDSHIPS: One of the wonderful aspects of being introverted is that we cherish intimate, deep relationships. We treasure time spent with one or two friends. Having a few true friends is so much more important than tallying dozens of virtual friends or tentative alliances. Don't let the popularity wars fool you. Value and cultivate your close relationships, and leave yourself open to finding new friends in unexpected places.

PARTNER WITH YOUR OPPOSITES: As introverts, we can learn so much from our more outgoing friends, classmates, and siblings. They can help us to grow as people and expand our comfort zones. Plus, extroverts can benefit from trying out our more quiet and contemplative style of living. We can forge rich and strong friendships. And when we partner together in the service of a cause or mission, we become that much more powerful, as our strengths balance one another's weaknesses.

HAVE FAITH IN YOURSELF: Although this might seem like a hard time to be quiet, stay strong. Remember that there are more of us introverts out there than you might think. A third to a half of the population is introverted, which means there are quite a few more kids like you making their way through those crowded, chaotic halls. As an introvert, you can accomplish anything.

FIND YOUR VOICE: I want to close with this excerpt from a college essay by Chloe, an introvert from Massachusetts, about coming to understand her quiet ways: "Finding my voice has involved finding out who I am. I believe that as I come to know myself better I find confidence, and with that comes a voice. Finding my voice is not just speaking more in class; it's finding a presence and discovering what I stand for and then standing up for it. It's learning that everything I say does not have to be perfect or even right. . . . The comfort that I found in my silences has fallen away. I can no longer just listen actively; I have to use my voice too. . . . I am slowly finding comfort in being uncomfortable and am beginning to like the sound of my own voice."

THE QUIET REVOLUTION IN THE CLASSROOM: AN AFTERWORD FOR TEACHERS

Shortly after the publication of *Quiet*, I received a note from a teacher at Greenwich Academy, a private girls' school in Connecticut. She had read the book the previous summer. It prompted her to look at many of her students through a new lens, and she decided that her school would benefit from a deeper understanding of the needs of introverted students. The teacher, Mrs. French, also oversaw one of several student research groups within the school. These girls would join together at the start of the year, choose a research project related to the lives of boys and girls, then go out and gather data on the subject. At the start of that school year, Mrs. French sat down with one of her groups and asked if any of the girls had ever been encouraged to participate more in class. The girls had a mix of personalities, but the quiet ones in the group immediately perked up. That one question sparked a discussion, and the girls quickly began working to find out more. Before long, they had decided they wanted to study what it was like to be an introvert at their school.

During the fall semester, they read portions of *Quiet*, viewed my TED Talk, and began planning their research. In January, they conducted a focus group of teachers. The teachers weren't aware of the topic, but once the girls started asking what it took to be a successful student, how the teachers viewed an ideal student, and other questions, the teachers realized that the girls were most curious about classroom participation. The focus group quickly turned into an open discussion, as the teachers began asking questions of their own.

When it became clear that the girls were focused on quiet students and their experiences in school, the teachers had very different responses. Some continued to insist that spoken participation was essential. Others wanted to learn more about introversion and potentially adjust their teaching style. They spoke about shifting from participation to engagement, as we discussed in chapter 2, and a few teachers shared the strategies they'd developed for quiet kids. For example, one teacher made a practice of approaching quiet kids privately, telling them the focus of the next class, and suggesting that they prepare something in advance. That way, if she called on them, they'd be ready.

After the focus group, the girls sent a survey to every student in the upper school, asking questions similar to the quiz at the start of this book. They discovered that roughly one-third of the girls at their school were introverted, as in the general population. With Mrs. French's help, they arranged to have *Quiet* placed on the staff's summer reading list.

When I visited the school some time later, I was struck by the impressive level of awareness about introverts and extroverts alike. The school hadn't been transformed, exactly. It still embraced the loud and crazy events that extroverts favor. On the first day of the year, for example, the school hosts a wild celebration for the new seniors, full of music, dancing, and primal screams. At the morning assembly, each senior runs down the auditorium aisle through a tunnel formed by their peers' outstretched arms. Then she steps to the podium and screams. That tradition was still intact when I visited. In fact, one of the girls in the research group, an extrovert named Madison, could not have been more excited about the prospect of all that madness. "I've had dreams about it!" she confessed with a laugh. "But my really good friend, a complete introvert, said, 'I don't hate it, but it's not my thing.'"

What impressed me was how well this school had taken into account both sets of needs. The teachers had begun to change their approach to participation in order to engage their quieter students, but none of these changes had come at the expense of the extroverted students. In fact, they benefited both types of kids. In one of Madison's classes, the teacher began insisting that the girls think for a minute before answering one of his questions. Madison admitted that she was usually eager to blurt something out immediately, whether it was right or wrong, but that the added time forced her to think more carefully.

These kinds of changes have begun at a number of schools across the country, and my colleagues and I plan to spread this Quiet Revolution even further. We're launching a pilot program for schools that want to "quietize" their curricula and school culture, and we'd love to talk to you about it. You can find more details about how to bring the Quiet Revolution to your school on our website, Quietrev.com. Please do get in touch—we would love to connect with you and your school!

In the meantime, here are three techniques for you to consider as you move from a model of classroom participation to engagement:

EMBRACE TECHNOLOGY

Many worry that online media can be a crutch, especially for students who aren't comfortable with live exchanges—but in fact it can be a bridge. Take the example of Michelle Lampinen, a high school English teacher in Freehold, New Jersey.

Lampinen has experimented with using Twitter and live chats while watching in-class movies of books the group has read. She has found—as many other teachers report—that kids who rarely raise their hands in a live class discussion readily add insights via the keyboard. One year, she also asked each of her students to create a blog, with ten entries that they wrote over the course of the year. She also required the students to comment intelligently on their classmates' blogs. This not only forced her students to read and process classmates' ideas, but also prompted in-person discussions that would not have taken place but for the intervention of online media.

BUILD IN THINKING TIME!

Jabiz Raisdana, a middle-school teacher in Singapore, once believed that spoken participation was essential. "I fell in that rut of thinking that people who are introverts or quiet need to be improved, so to speak," he admitted. Then a student led him to change both his attitude and his process. "I had this one student," he recalled, "and he was an amazingly talented filmmaker and super-super-introverted."

The boy never spoke in class. For the first few days of school, Mr. Raisdana tried to encourage him to participate, asking for his opinion on a given subject. During the second week of class, the student finally spoke up. "I don't have anything that

I feel I have to say right now," he began. "When I do, I will, so until then, please leave me alone."

Mr. Raisdana wasn't offended; he was floored. "I'm sitting there thinking, 'This thirteen-year-old kid just owned me!'" Now, that student was—shall we say—a little direct, and most teachers would probably not be as understanding when spoken to in that way. Yet Mr. Raisdana listened because the boy summarized the essential problem so perfectly: He didn't see the point of speaking just to speak. And although the boy didn't raise his hand, he consistently turned in very thoughtful, well-written assignments. Through his work he showed that he was listening to and absorbing every single word in class. He was a model student. Just a really, really quiet one.

The boy inspired Mr. Raisdana to rethink the way he evaluated participation. "Just because they're not saying anything doesn't mean they're not engaged in the material," the teacher realized. "It's often the kids who are blabbing on and on who just want to hear themselves talk and really don't know what they want to talk *about*." Mr. Raisdana found that he had a number of introverted kids in his class, so he changed his teaching method. He would start out with a topic of discussion, but instead of calling on kids right away, he asked them to write out their ideas on the subject. After the writing time, the kids would take another few minutes to read what their classmates had written, and add comments if they had something to say. "Then we would go have our discussion," Mr.

Raisdana said. "The kids had already thought about it. They'd already written and read what other people had said, and in that way it wasn't a cold turkey discussion." The mix of writing, reading, commentary, and class discussion amplified the voices of the quiet kids. Mr. Raisdana didn't force anyone to participate during the open discussion, but often the introverted kids would anyway.

Introversion should not be seen as an excuse to remain silent, of course. Ideally, young people should try to stretch themselves and raise their hands now and then; after all, they'll have to do some version of this during their adult lives too. Kavan Yee, a high school teacher in Washington, D.C., was very sensitive to the needs of his quiet kids, but he also believed that it was important for these students to become comfortable speaking in class. He let them know before class that he was going to ask their opinion on a particular question. He selected questions that he knew—from their work or private conversations—would interest his students, and increase their chances for success. "You should be able to sit amongst a group of your peers and give a presentation or articulate your ideas," says Mr. Yee. "But I tell the students it's *their* process, and their pace."

BREAK THE CLASS INTO SMALL DISCUSSION GROUPS

Often, the same student who wouldn't be comfortable addressing an entire classroom will find his or her voice in a small group or with a single trusted partner. That's why I'm a strong proponent of the Think/Pair/Share technique described in chapter 2. These can be great opportunities for the introverted kids in your classroom to express their ideas.

A GUIDE FOR PARENTS

This is a book for and about young readers, but I suspect that some parents may skim these pages as well. The school years can be challenging for introverts—and for their parents too. The most important advice I can offer is to help your quiet children to draw on their own natural strengths—as listeners, observers, thinkers, and quietly determined doers. It's our role as parents to help our children grow, and to explore their limits, while also making sure to honor, and take delight, in who they actually are. As Eleanor, the mother of an introverted teen boy, puts it: "It's more important for introverted kids to show that you're on their team. They need more team members than the normal teens—people who really know them."

If you're interested in learning more about how to parent your quiet teen, Quiet Revolution is launching a series of interactive, multimedia master classes designed expressly for parents like you. These classes will give you the parenting tools you need; the scripts to advocate for your child with teachers and well-meaning friends and relatives who comment on his or her quiet ways; and an online forum for interacting with other parents of quiet children. You'll be able to swap stories, ask for and give advice, and build a support network with moms and dads who are facing similar rewards and challenges with their own quiet children. If you're interested in learning more, please feel free to visit Parenting.quietrev.com.

In the meantime, here are a few simple strategies you can start to use right away.

ENCOURAGE MASTERY AND SELF-EXPRESSION

The value of mastery and self-expression for any child can't be overstated, but introverted kids in particular should be encouraged to find an outlet, whether on the playing field, a stage, a lab, an extracurricular activity, or a simple piece of paper. Introverts tend to be driven by their interests and passions, naturally organizing their lives around the things they love most to do. This is a great boon, because focusing on one or two pursuits tends to build mastery in a given area, and mastery builds self-confidence—rather than the other way around. Many introverted kids also find friends through their shared passions, rather than by socializing for its own sake. In the name of their passions, some kids even find themselves ascending to leadership positions they wouldn't otherwise have dreamed of.

As a parent, one of the best things you can do is to simply get out of the way. Make sure your child is exposed to many different subjects and pursuits—and then let him or her go. Don't expect your child's passions to ignite instantly. Developing and cultivating enthusiasms can be the work of a lifetime, but it's well worth the wait.

HELP YOUR CHILD TO NAVIGATE SOCIAL LIFE

Let's face it: Adolescence + social life can be a rocky road—and all the more so for introverted kids, who are usually living in school cultures in which being gregarious and outgoing is the most highly valued currency. As a loving parent, you'll likely be eager to help your child navigate these waters. Before you plunge in, though, it helps to remember that you'll likely face different challenges as a parent, depending on whether you're an introvert or an extrovert yourself.

If you're an introvert, you can probably empathize easily with your child's experiences, but you may sometimes feel those struggles *too* vicariously. If this describes you, you may need to do some inner work of your own—whether with a friend, a therapist, or through meditation—to learn to love your quiet self, and to realize that your child is a different person who is not destined to repeat the same painful experiences you may have weathered during your own adolescence.

If you're an extrovert, in contrast, you may have the advantage of being able to provide your child a role model of an easygoing approach to social life. But you may struggle to relate to your child's inner experiences and concerns. Extroverted parents are often mystified by their introverted child's apparent lack of interest in parties and other social engagements.

The trick is often to find a happy medium between a hands-off and hands-on approach to your child's social life. If your child shows signs of being in trouble or wanting to talk, then by all means be there for him or her; it can often help to role-play a difficult social situation at the kitchen table the night before your child has to enact it at the school cafeteria. But do know that psychologists such as Kenneth Rubin at the University of Maryland have found that as long as kids have one or two close friends, they have all the indicators they need for a happy future. They absolutely don't need to be part of a large and gregarious band of friends—even if that kind of social life made you happy during your own adolescence. Many introverts form a small number of strong and loyal friendships throughout their childhood and adult years. "Remember that if you have one true friend, you're luckier than anyone else in the world, because it's so hard to have a true friendship," says the psychologist Vidisha Patel. "If you have that one true friend, you're doing really, really well."

PREPARE FOR ORAL PRESENTATIONS

Some introverts are very comfortable with public speaking. If your child is one of them, more power to her! But if your child is one of the many with stage fright—public speaking is the world's most common phobia, afflicting extroverts as well as introverts—here are some ways to help him overcome it:

MONITOR ANXIETY LEVELS: It's great to ask your child to step outside her comfort zone—but she needs to do so within manageable anxiety levels. Ask how anxious she is on a scale of 1 to 10. You want her to be in the 4 to 6 range. The 7 to 10 range approaches panic and carries too high a risk of being unpleasant and counterproductive. Lower than 4 is a sign that she might be coasting. The zone of growth is 4 to 6. Once she's mastered a given task within this zone, she can try successively more challenging forms of performance.

RESEARCH: Encourage your child to master the subject he'll be presenting, whether it's a book, a news topic, or a famous historical figure. Remember that mastery breeds confidence, not the other way around!

BRAINSTORM: Offer a whiteboard, chalkboard, or even a large piece of paper for jotting down a list of key facts or ideas.

DISCUSS: Interview your child about the topic in a friendly way; he or she might find a particular area of focus just through the conversation, and this will be a first bit of practice in presenting the topic out loud.

OUTLINE AND PREPARE: Next, your child should be ready to identify the main points of the presentation, assemble the appropriate visual aids, if allowed, and even write out the full presentation when appropriate.

REHEARSE: Whether you use dolls, toys, or family members, make sure that your child practices the presentation repeatedly at home or in a small, trusted group. Remind your child to smile and make eye contact with a few different people, and to breathe for relaxation.

CULTIVATE A RESTORATIVE NICHE

Giving introverts the quiet time they need is the key to their emotional health and success at school, discovered the mom of an introverted young woman named Rupal. When Rupal was in kindergarten, her mother picked her up from school every day. Each day Rupal beamed and smiled as she walked out of class—but once inside the car, she erupted at the slightest problem. Her mother would try to figure out how she had erred. Had she given Rupal the wrong juice box? Packed the wrong snack? Dressed her in the wrong shoes? Meanwhile, Rupal would cry and scream and transform into a miniature tornado.

Her mother and father were not at all used to this behavior—their daughter had always been a pleasure. They worried that Rupal was acting this way at school too, so they asked her teacher about her behavior. To their surprise and relief, the teacher told them that Rupal was an absolute delight.

That's when Rupal's mother realized how hard her daughter had to work at school each day simply to keep it together and to interact with the other kids and her teacher. By the end of the day, she was emotionally exhausted. Once the door to their minivan closed, she let it all out on the one person she could: her mother.

Rupal outgrew those tantrums, but her mother never forgot them. She understood that her daughter needed time to recover from the long, social days at school. As Rupal grew older, she shed the temper tantrums and adopted a new coping mechanism. Each day she came home from school, marched straight to her room with little more than a word to her mother, and stayed there for an hour or more, reading, listening to music, and writing. She would emerge revived and ready to interact. For her mother, these moments could be painful. But she knew how badly her daughter needed them.

As Rupal's mom's experience shows us, these episodes are not always easy. We want to interact with our children after school; we want to see them interacting with their peers at extracurricular activities. But we need to be careful to distinguish our needs from theirs. This doesn't mean that your introverted child will spend his entire adolescence alone in his bedroom. But it does mean that respecting his need for a little alone time can give him the break he needs in order to meet the rest of his day feeling happier, more energized, and more present and available to those around him. Introverted kids "need time to decompress and daydream and do absolutely nothing, regardless of what comes out of that nothing," says the psychologist Elizabeth Mika. "We should schedule daydreaming into their extracurriculars."

ACKNOWLEDGMENTS

With huge and heartfelt thanks to Gonzo, Sam, and Eli, my daily joy and inspiration; to my co-authors, Greg Mone and Erica Moroz, without whom this book could not exist; to my wise and intrepid editor, Lauri Hornik, who saw this book through so many twists and turns; to my superb agent, Richard Pine; to the wonderful team at Penguin: Anton Abrahamsen, Regina Castillo, Christina Colangelo, Rachel Cone-Gorham, Lauren Donovan, Jackie Engel, Felicia Frazier, Carmela Iaria, Jen Loja, Shanta Newlin, Vanessa Robles, Jasmin Rubero, Kristen Tozzo, Irene Vandervoort, and Don Weisberg; to Grant Snider, for his elegant illustrations; to President Renee Coale, for everything; and most of all, to all the many people who shared your stories and your wisdom in interviews for this book.

And with special thanks to the talented and passionate

people, too many to be named, who helped and are helping to build Quiet Revolution.

Last but not least: To all the quiet kids, teens, parents, caregivers, and educators who reached out to me over the past years since the adult version of *Quiet* was published—it was you, most of all, who inspired me to write this book.

NOTES

INTRODUCTION

p. 5 **Introverts make up a third to half of the population:** Rowan Bayne, in *The Myers-Briggs Type Indicator: A Critical Review and Practical Guide* (London: Chapman and Hall, 1995).

p. 7 **Carl Jung:** Carl G. Jung, *Psychological Types* (Princeton, NJ: Princeton University Press, 1971; originally published in German as *Psychologische Typen* [Zurch: Rascher Verlag, 1921]), see esp. 330–337.

p. 11 **Gandhi:** *Gandhi: An Autobiography: The Story of My Experiments with Truth* (Boston Beacon Press, 1957), esp. 6, 20, 40–41, 59–62, 90–91.

pp. 11–12 **Kareem Abdul-Jabbar:** Kareem Abdul-Jabbar, "20 Things I Wish I'd Known When I Was 30," *Esquire*, April 30, 2013. http://www.esquire.com/blogs/news/kareem-things-i-wish-i-knew

p. 12 **Beyoncé:** Elisa Lipsky-Karasz, "Beyoncé's Baby Love: The Extended Interview," *Harper's Bazaar*, October 11, 2011. http://www.harpersbazaar.com/celebrity/latest/news/a7436/beyonce-q-and-a-101111/

p. 12 **Emma Watson:** Derek Blasberg, "The Bloom of the Wallflower," *Wonderland* magazine, February 5, 2014. http://www.wonderlandmagazine.com/2014/02/the-bloom-of-the-wallflower-by-derek-blasberg/

pp.12–13 **Misty Copeland:** Rivka Galchen, "An Unlikely Ballerina," *The New Yorker,* September 22, 2014. http://www.newyorker.com/magazine/2014/09/22/unlikely-ballerina.

p.13 **Albert Einstein:** Walter Isaacson, *Einstein: His Life and Universe* (New York: Simon & Schuster, 2007), 4, 12, 17, 2, 31, etc.

CHAPTER 1

p. 22 **Hans Eysenck's lemon juice study:** Hans J. Eysenck, *Genius: The Natural History of Creativity* (New York: Cambridge University Press, 1995).

p. 23 **Russell Geen:** "Preferred Stimulation Levels in Introverts and Extroverts: Effects on Arousal and Performance," *Journal of Personality and Social Psychology* 46, no. 6 (1984): 1303–1312. http://psycnet.apa.org/psycinfo/1984-28698-001.

pp. 25–26 **Chelsea Grefe:** Interview with the author.

CHAPTER 2

p. 36 **Rethinking Class Participation:** Teachers aren't the only ones who reward outspoken participation. Studies suggest that we *all* think highly of talkative group members. A group of scientists once divided college students into groups and asked them to solve a series of math problems together. While the students were working out the answers, the scientists observed them. Once the groups settled on their answers, the scientists asked them privately to rate the other members of their group. On the whole, the students who spoke often and early received the highest ratings from their peers and were considered the smartest—even though the talkers didn't perform as well on the tests!

Cameron Anderson and Gavin J. Kilduff, "Why Do Dominant Personalities Attain Influence in Face-to-Face Groups? The Competence Signaling Effects of Trait Dominance," *Journal of Personality and Social Psychology* 96, no. 2 (2009): 491–503.

p. 37 **Mary Budd Rowe:** Mary Budd Rowe, "Wait-Time: Slowing Down May Be a Way of Speeding Up," *Journal of Teacher Education* 37, no. 1 (January 1986).

p. 38 **Emily,** from an e-mail to the author on June 10, 2013.

p. 42 **Liam** is an amalgam of two boys interviewed by the author (name has been changed).

CHAPTER 3

pp. 51–52 **Adam Grant:** A. M. Grant, F. Gino, D. A. Hofmann, "Reversing the Extraverted Leadership Advantage: The Role of Employee Proactivity," *Academy of Management Journal* 54, no. 3 (2011): 528–550.

p. 52 **Jim Collins:** Jim Collins, *Good to Great: Why Some Companies Make the Leap—and Others Don't* (New York: HarperCollins, 2001).

CHAPTER 4

p. 63 **Eileen Fisher:** From Eileen's Facebook page (https://www.facebook.com/EILEENFISHERNY/posts/376227809077218).

pp. 64–66 **Eleanor Roosevelt:** Blanche Wiesen Cook, *Eleanor Roosevelt, Volume One: 1884–1933* (New York: Viking Penguin, 1992), *125–236. Also, The American Experience: Eleanor Roosevelt* (Public Broadcasting System, Ambrica Productions, 2000). See transcript: http://pbs.org/wgbh/amex/eleanor/filmmore/transcript/transcript1.html.

CHAPTER 5

p. 88 **Ira Glass:** Kathryn Schulz, "On Air and On Error: This American Life's Ira Glass on Being Wrong," Slate.com, June 7, 2010. http://www.slate.com/content/slate/blogs/thewrongstuff/2010/06/07/on_air_and_on_error_this_american_life_s_ira_glass_on_being_wrong.html

CHAPTER 7

p. 112 **psychologists have been trying to figure out whether people act the same way online as they do in real life:** Samuel D. Gosling, Ph.D., Adam A. Augustine, M.S., Simine Vazire, Ph.D., Nicholas Holtzman, M.A., and Sam Gaddis, B.S., "Manifestations of Personality in Online Social Networks: Self-Reported Facebook-Related Behaviors and Observable Profile Information" *Cyberpsychology, Behavior, and Social Networking* 14, no. 9 (2011). http://www.ncbi.nlm.nih.gov/pmc/articles/PMC3180765/pdf/cyber.2010.0087.pdf

p. 112 **The scientists questioned 126 high school students about how they engaged with one another:** "Friending, IMing, and Hanging Out Face-to-Face: Overlap in Adolescents' Online and Offline Social Networks," S. M. Reich, K. Subrahmanyam, G. Espinoza, *Dev Psychol*, no. 2 (March 2012): 356–368. http://www.ncbi.nlm.nih.gov/pubmed/22369341.

pp. 113–14 **Aimee Yermish:** Interview with author.

p. 115 **those with high friend counts were often happier with their lives:** A. M. Manago, T. Taylor, P. M. Greenfield, "Me and My 400 Friends: the Anatomy of College Students' Facebook Networks, Their Communication Patterns, and Well-Being," *Dev Psychol*, Epub (Jan 30, 2012). http://www.ncbi.nlm.nih.gov/pubmed/22288367.

CHAPTER 8

Steve Wonzniak: The story of Stephen Wozniak throughout this chapter is drawn largely from his autobiography, *iWoz* (New York: W. W. Norton, 2006). The description of Woz as being the "nerd soul" of Apple comes from http://valleywag.gawker.com/220602/wozniak-jobs-design-role-overstated.

pp. 130–31 **a psychologist named Avril Thorne set up an experiment:** Avril Thorne, "The Press of Personality: A Study of Conversations Between Introverts and Extraverts," *Journal of Personality and Social Psychology* 53, no. 4 (1987): 718–726.

CHAPTER 9

p. 136–137 Interview of J. K. Rowling by Shelagh Rogers and Lauren McCormick, Canadian Broadcasting Corp., October 26, 2000.

p. 137 **John Green:** "Thoughts from Places: The Tour," Nerdfighteria Wiki, January 17, 2012.

p. 141 **Pete Docter:** Jen Lacey, "Inside Out, Buzz Lightyear and the Introverted Director, Pete Docter," ABC.net, June17, 2015. http://blogs.abc.net.au/nsw/2015/06/pixar-director-pete-docter-.html. Also, Michael O' Sullivan, "'Up' Director Finds Escape in Reality," *The Washington Post*, May, 29, 2009. http://www.washingtonpost.com/wp-dyn/content/article/2009/05/28/AR2009052801064.html

p. 142 **Conrad Tao:** Justin Davidson, "The Vulnerable Age," *New York* magazine, March 25, 2012. http://nymag.com/arts/classicaldance/classical/profiles/conrad-tao-2012-4/

p. 143 **Mihaly Csikszentmihalyi:** Mihaly Csikszentmihalyi, *Creativity: Flow and the Psychology of Discovery and Invention* (New York: Harper Perennial, 2013), p.177.

CHAPTER 10

p. 154 **Alan Goldberg:** Interview with the author, July 24, 2013.

p. 155 **Washington Nationals:** Thomas Boswell, "Washington Nationals Have Right Personality to Handle the Long Grind of a Regular Season," *The Washington Post*, February 17, 2013. https://www.washingtonpost.com/sports/nationals/washington-nationals-have-right-personality-to-handle-the-long-grind-of-a-regular-season/2013/02/17/fd77dfae-793f-11e2-82e8-61a46c2cde3d_story.html.

CHAPTER 11

p.161–64 **Jessica Watson:** Jessica Watson, *True Spirit: The True Story of a 16-Year-Old Australian Who Sailed Solo, Nonstop, and Unassisted*

Around the World (New York: Atria Books, 2010). And her website, http://www.jessicawatson.com.au/about-jessica.

p. 165 **researchers looked at introverts and extroverts who won gambling contests:** Michael X. Cohen et. al, "Individual Differences in Extroversion and Dopamine Genetics Predict Neural Reward Responses," *Cognitive Brain Research* 25 (2005): 851–861.

p. 166 **Breivik examined the personalities of the members of a 1985 Norwegian expedition to Mount Everest:** Interview with the author, January 16, 2014. Also, G. Breivik, "Personality, Sensation Seeking and Risk Taking Among Everest Climbers," *International Journal of Sport Psychology* 27, no. 3 (1996): pp. 308–320.

p. 167–68 **Charles Darwin:** The Darwin material is from http://darwin-online.org.uk/content/frameset?viewtype=text&itemID=F1497 &pageseq=1, and Charles Darwin, *Voyage of the Beagle* (New York: Penguin Classics, Abridged edition, 1989)

CHAPTER 12
p. 176–178 **Rosa Parks:** *Rosa Parks: A Life (New York: Penguin, 2000).*

CHAPTER 13
p. 195 **Steve Martin:** Steve Hinds, "Steve Martin: Wild and Crazy Introvert," www.quietrev.com, http://www.quietrev.com/steve -martin-wild-and-crazy-introvert/

p. 195 **Emma Watson:** Tavi Gevinson, "I Want It to Be Worth It: An Interview With Emma Watson," *Rookie* magazine, May 27, 2013. http://www.rookiemag.com/2013/05/emma-watson-interview/

p. 198 **Free Trait Theory:** For an overview of Free Trait Theory, see Brian R. Little, "Free Traits, Personal Projects, and Idio-Tapes: Three Tiers for Personality Psychology," *Psychological Inquiry* 7, no. 4 (1996): pp. 340–344.

Brian Little: The stories about Brian Little throughout this chapter come from numerous telephone and e-mail interviews with the author between 2006 and 2010.

CHAPTER 14

p. 208 "Restorative Niche": Brian Little, "Free Traits and Personal Contexts: Expanding a Social Ecological Model of Well-Being," in *Person Environment Psychology: New Directions and Perspectives*, edited by W. Bruce Walsh et. al. (Mahwah, NJ: Lawrence Erlbaum Associates, 2000).

p. 212 **The scientists found that a desire for solitude was frowned upon among the middle-school kids:** Jennifer M. Wang, Kenneth H. Rubin, Brett Laursen, Cathryn Booth-LaForce, Linda Rose-Krasnor, "Preference-for-Solitude and Adjustment Difficulties in Early and Late Adolescence," *Journal of Clinical Child & Adolescent Psychology* 0 (0) (2013): 1–9, 2013 http://www.academia.edu/3630522 /Preference-for-Solitude_and_Adjustment_Difficulties_in_Early_ and_Late_Adolescence

INDEX

ABOUT THE AUTHOR

Susan Cain prefers listening to talking, reading to socializing, and cozy chats to group settings. She likes to think before she speaks. She dreams big and has audacious goals, and she sees no contradiction between this and her quiet nature.

A graduate of Princeton University and Harvard Law School, Cain is the cofounder of Quiet Revolution and the author of the *New York Times* bestseller *Quiet*, which has been translated into 40 languages and spent over four years on the bestseller list. Her record-smashing TED Talk has been viewed more than twelve million times. She has received Harvard Law School's Celebration Award for Thought Leadership, the Toastmasters International Golden Gavel Award, and was named one of the world's Top 50 Leadership and Management Experts by *Inc.* magazine. She lives in the Hudson River Valley with her husband and two sons.